Guideposts for Banking Expansion

The Rutgers Banking Series consists of books in the field of American banking which have grown out of research at the Stonier Graduate School of Banking.

Guideposts for Banking Expansion

by Gavin Spofford

Rutgers University Press · *New Brunswick, New Jersey*

To the memory of my brother

ENSIGN DONALD E. SPOFFORD, USNR

For yours would have been a valuable contribution

Contents

I **Introduction** 3

Changes in Banking
Economic Feasibility
Nonstatistical Aspects
Ingress without Egress

II **Postwar Growth—Banking and the Economy** 9

Near Banking: Savings and Loan Associations and
    Credit Unions
New Offices vs. The Economy
Area Characteristics
Categories of New Offices

III **The Banking System and Its Supervisory Authorities** 23

Changing Perspectives
The Dual System—History
The Dual System—Supervision

IV **Measuring Deposit Potential** 45

Background Data
Types of Cases

Basic Source Materials
Deposit Potential
Caution

V   New Branch Cases   65

The New Shopping Center Case
The Savings Institution Case
The Strategic Access Case
The Limited Service Facility

VI   Negative Branch Cases   84

The No-Room-for-Three Case
The Underdeveloped Community Case

VII   Successful New Banks   89

Bank G
Bank G—Hypothetical Comparison
Bank H
Bank H—Hypothetical Comparison

VIII   New Banks—Refused Charters   103

Case I
Case I—Hypothetical Comparison
Case J
Case J—Hypothetical Comparison

IX   Do It Yourself   115

Don't Do It Yourself
The Questions
Sampling and Substance
The Business of Averages
Actual vs. Potential
The Use of Knowledge

X *Conclusions* 139

Individual Bank Analysis
Expansion Analysis
Comments on Deposits
The Aggregate View

Appendix I 149

Appendix II 153

Appendix III 156

Appendix IV 158

Appendix V 162

Appendix VI 167

Appendix VII 170

Appendix VIII 175

Appendix IX 180

Notes 185

Bibliography 188

Foreword

Banking has been aptly described as the handmaiden to industry and trade. Any major change affecting the economy as a whole is bound to be reflected in banking developments.

The changes that have occurred in the economy of the country since the end of World War II have been manifold and dynamic. Living standards have risen. There has been a constant shift from the farm to the city. New suburbs were developed and the demand for credit on the part of the people increased materially.

The response of the banks to these developments was a pronounced merger movement, a desire for branches in order to follow the people to their new homes, and an effort to provide credit based not only on self-liquidating transactions, but also on the earning power of the individual.

The resources of the banks reflect the general rise in the gross national product and national income. These changes in the economy and in banking have created a number of problems for the banker which cannot be solved by the rule of thumb. Careful investigation, study, and experience are necessary to solve these problems satisfactorily and to avoid grief and loss.

Guideposts for Banking Expansion by Gavin Spofford, assistant vice president of the Hanover Bank, endeavors to throw light on these problems and difficulties and offers highly useful information to the practical banker. Mr. Spofford's analysis is the more valuable since it is based on a thorough theoretical knowledge of economics in general and banking in particular, combined with practical experience gained throughout the past few years as a bank officer. His work will be of considerable interest to students of banking in general and to the practical banker in particular.

MARCUS NADLER

Guideposts for Banking Expansion

1

Introduction

This book arose out of some experience in assisting banks in planning for and measuring the potential of new office locations. It was altogether too evident that there was little but guesswork to rely on and that a major industry was undergoing substantial expansion without any guideposts to measure the fate of such investments as it was making. A challenge of this type was worthy of the effort, especially the plunge into a new and undeveloped field. The results, as written here, are frustratingly fractional, which was predictable. One conclusion was reached, however, which has brought the effort full circle to its starting point: each investigation must be individual as to its raw material and as to the conversion of that raw material into useful estimates. Contained herein, then, are suggestions as to method and source of data which it is hoped will be of aid in those investigations.

It soon became evident that there is an over-all concern of economic soundness as well as an individual one of profitability. Both are considered in some detail. The general approach has been to start with an aggregate view of the recent past plus a discernment of some of the evident and important trends. From this there developed a discussion of the status of banking in relation to the supervisory authorities which, perforce, play an integral role in banking expansion. The study then proceeds into the knowledge to be gained from a variety of specific cases and concludes with an attempted description of proper methods of self-analysis. It is appropriate to start with the aggregate view.

The pattern of economic life in the United States has undergone astounding changes since the end of World War II. More important, the trends which have caused that pattern shift are themselves constantly changing. The one certain element of the past fifteen years which will also hold during the next fifteen is population growth. The composition of that population, by occupation, location of residence, income and spending habits, and the evolving application of monetary and fiscal policy are the trends to be watched. A trend, in this instance a mass change in economic habit, follows a fairly typical curve: slow start, acceleration to a position of dominance, a flattening out, and a subsequent decline of varying proportions depending on what new trends come along to substitute for or supplant it. Economic life is the interweaving of such trends, much as the waves of the sea, but the analogy parts from the illustration here, for the level of the economic sea can be raised or lowered by the effects of its waves on one another. There are three such trends which played an important role in the economic development of the postwar period, the description of which will give some illustration of possible future changes which will effect banking as well as many other facets of our economy:

1. The shift in the distribution of personal income. From the barest beginning with the income tax in 1913, this trend accelerated during the thirties and achieved unheard-of levels during World War II. The trend may be said to have flattened somewhat since the war, with conflicting minor changes. It is politically unlikely to be reversed and more likely to be further increased, although at a declining rate. Further, there

is unprovable evidence that the so-called lower classes are in possession of far more liquid wealth than is generally realized. A comparison of the aggregate interest paid on savings to the amount reported for income tax purposes shows a sizeable discrepancy. Aside from its economic or political implications, this is a further refinement within a trend which deserves bankers' attention.

2. The changing location of people's residences. Desertion of the farm for the city is a well-known political lament. From over half the total population in 1910, current estimates leave only about 10 per cent of a much larger population on the farms today. But this is only a contributing element in the much more important trend toward the major urban area type of economic complex. The so-called concentric ring development of urban areas is the foremost reality of current economic activity. Balance is the major problem in such complexes—regarding taxes, marketing, transportation, and in many other respects. The periphery is booming, and established institutions are vying for representation. This is the rising part of the trend and its meaning for banks will occupy much of what is to be said later. But already there is a countertrend rising behind it in the form of urban renewal activities. So long as these complexes retain an important center or core, distance will be a factor fighting the expansion and heightening the pressure for urban and closer suburban renewal. This trend and the changes in income distribution make an interesting combination for bankers.

3. The shifting allocation of discretionary saving. In the larger sense, saving includes all dollars not spent for consumption purposes. This includes the short-term inventory of dollars held in checking accounts by individuals and corporations as well as savings accounts, savings and loan shares, bonds, mutual funds, life insurance and other more permanent types of investment.

The development of "near money," or corporate and individual investment in short-term interest-bearing obligations of moneys *which would otherwise* be held in checking accounts, is a tight money phenomenon of the past few years. To be sure, it happened before, as in the twenties, and there is no assurance that it will continue. Here, too, the trend would appear to have reached the flattening-out stage. Such investments are a direct, if not straight-line, function of money rates; therefore, future levels of money rates are of paramount importance. In this regard, the fact that the United States, for the first time in this century, has to keep an eye on its gold supply provides one important clue regardless of prevailing political sentiment. Near money is of greatest concern to larger banks with a significant corporate business, but its effects are felt throughout the banking system. This is a trend to watch.

The second half of the shift in relative shares is of even greater dollar importance. In round totals, dollar deposits in U.S. banks, including savings banks, approximate $255 billion. Of this, about $152 billion is in demand balances, the remainder is savings of which savings banks have approximately $40 billion. These figures represent an increase of a little under $60 billion since the war. Against this, the savings and loan associations and the credit unions have come almost from nowhere to positions of $55 billion and $5 billion, respectively. Mutual funds are legion, and the insurance companies are making new efforts to attract the consumer dollar. This, too, is a trend for the banking industry to watch.

CHANGES IN BANKING

Much of the economic ferment described above has already been reflected in changed and changing banking practices. Ever since the victory of Andrew Jackson over the Second Bank of the United States in 1836 there has been strong popular sentiment for the local independent bank and against any form of monopoly, either private or federal. The enactment of the Federal Reserve System in 1913 was possible only after prolonged, bitter experience, and even that was a compromise—twelve central banks instead of one. Hindsight comment about the depression and its causes laid much of the blame on the existence of far too many individual banks which were too small, too weak, and too poorly supervised. Not even the Banking Acts of 1933 and 1935 were able to break down this area of state sovereignty and the sentiment for local independent operation.

Against this reticence there has been steady economic and political pressure since World War II. Each new economic center that has been created or promoted, has carried with it some sentiment for a banking facility. Much of this interest is satiated or blunted, as the case may be, by the establishment of a branch of an existing bank. However, branch banking in many areas is not the solution either by law or by sentiment. The relative virtues of a new independent bank versus a branch will not be debated here, but some indications of their economic feasibility and their actual accomplishments will be considered as individual cases later. Formation of such new units, banks or branches, as well as savings and loan offices constitute the major evidences of physical changes in banking in the recent past, and as such, together with the overlying trends, should give some indication of future developments.

ECONOMIC FEASIBILITY

An effort will be made through the investigation of available aggregate statistics and through examination of some representative cases of new branches and of new unit banks to determine some of the economic bench marks by which the success of a new banking office can be estimated in advance. This study will be confined primarily to estimates of deposit potential based on availability of comparable data. The fields of physical equipment, loan potential, earnings, break-even points, asset allocation, and other closely related aspects of new bank formation, although important, are derivative of this basic resource. However, it is hoped that, since deposits are the life-blood of any bank, the information developed here will provide useful correlation to other studies covering the over-all subject.

NONSTATISTICAL ASPECTS

Demonstration of economic strength is only the second most important factor in consideration of a new bank charter or branch permit. The central point in determining the desirability of granting a new bank charter or branch permit is the character of the people who will control and operate the institution. In both of its major endeavors, providing a safe depositary and in lending money, a bank automatically assumes a heavy responsibility. There are several sets of economic circumstances under which interest in the formation of a new bank charter or branch permit can develop. Therefore, it is essential to know the motives and interests of the organizers, which may range from public pride to indirect profit. It is and should be the mandate of chartering authorities to be inherently skeptical in this regard. This is the most important facet of new bank decisions which by its nature cannot be considered here except to the extent of outlining some of the expected standards.

INGRESS WITHOUT EGRESS

A crucial factor in determining the economic feasibility of a new unit bank charter or branch permit is the quasi-public nature of such an institution. A bank can discontinue business only at the cost of considerable upset to the economy that it serves. Consequently, a margin of safety greater than required in most new private enterprises is essential.

II

Postwar growth—
banking and the economy

In recent years applications for new branch permits and new bank charters have jumped substantially. Many institutions have cast about in this direction, frequently for no other reason than a desire to keep up with the times. A second and increasingly important reason for branch consideration is to defend existing business in an area where a competitor might establish a facility. The third and most solid base is the logical desire to obtain the new business that accompanies real new growth in some subarea of the bank's natural trade area.

For all these reasons banks are scrutinizing their trade areas with varying degrees of analytical acumen. Many of them and many new unit bank organizing groups subsequently submit applications to the appropriate supervisory authorities. Both approvals and refusals have increased steadily in recent years. Refusals have increased in greater absolute degree due to both increasing competition among existing offices and more vigorous opposition to new applications.[1] Uncountable, of course, are the considerations which never reach the supervisory authorities, nor is there any known tabulation of applications submitted. Suffice to say that the margin of guesswork is steadily diminishing and that realistic, well-founded research will be a necessity in the future, as it has not always been heretofore.

It is now appropriate to review the changes in banking offices since World War II. As of December 31, 1940, there were 15,120 main banking offices with 3,665 branches. Totals in that and subsequent years are given in Table 1.[2]

Table 1

BANKS AND POPULATION DENSITY[2]

Date	Main Banks	Branches	Total	Population Per Office
Dec. 1940	15,120	3,665	18,785	7,003
Dec. 1945	14,744	3,937	18,681	7,494
Dec. 1950	14,699	5,020	19,719	7,769
Dec. 1955	14,320	7,258	21,578	7,728
Dec. 1957	14,149	8,556	22,705	7,579
Dec. 1958	14,075	9,177	23,252	7,498
Dec. 1959	14,004	10,238	24,242	7,407

While the number of offices has grown substantially, branch banking still covers a minority portion of the banking facilities in the United States. Further, the pattern is uneven, largely because of varying state laws. California, the best-known state in terms of state-wide branching, had 1,400 branches of 131 main banks as of mid-1958. New York State, which until recently allowed branching within limited districts, had 1,923 branches of 583 main banks at the same date. Pennsylvania, with branching allowed in contiguous counties, had 759 main banks (the largest number in any state) with 670 branches. By contrast, Illinois, Texas, and Florida, among others, allowed no branching whatever. As a generalization, the philosophy of branch banking is further advanced along the seaboards than in the interior of the country.

In the most recent survey—as of June 30, 1949—over 70 per cent of banks having branches had only one or two, and 94 per cent of these operated branches only within the head office county or contiguous counties. In total, 1,162 banks, less than 10 per cent of all banks, operated a total of 4,386 branches. This was approximately 30 per cent of all banking offices versus approximately 25 per cent in 1939. During this period the total number of banks declined slightly while the number of branches increased by 889.[3]

Since the date of this survey the number of unit banks has continued to decline steadily, while the number of new branches and of new unit banks has jumped sharply. Table 2 shows the establishment of new branches and new banks in the postwar era, as approved by the Federal Deposit Insurance Corporation.

Table 2 [4]

NEW BRANCHES AND BANKS IN
THE POSTWAR PERIOD

Year	New Branches *	New Banks
1946	214	132
1947	208	99
1948	211	62
1949	247	61
1950	300	59
1951	345	53
1952	349	62
1953	407	59
1954	550	66
1955	677	103
1956	728	107
1957	671	85
1958	716	92
1959	745	115
	6,368	1,155

* These figures include some savings bank offices. The number of individual savings banks has changed only nominally in some years, however.

NEAR BANKING: SAVINGS AND LOAN ASSOCIATIONS AND CREDIT UNIONS

The figures on activity in the commercial and savings banking fields are by no means the entire story. To set the background of banking growth in the postwar period properly the activities in the savings and loan association and credit union fields must also be considered. It might be said, perhaps, that other types of institutions, such as mutual funds and insurance companies, should be included as competitors for the public's dollars but these latter are in the investment category. Banking and near banking is here defined as including those institutions into which the public places its money under the impression that it is making a deposit the principal amount of which will be unchanged and can be got back on demand. Much has been said about the variations between types of institutions in these crucial respects but the fact remains that these are the public expectations when they make such deposits or buy such shares. As such, the market determinants are similar if not duplicating and are worthy of joint review.

Table 3

TOTAL NUMBER OF BANKING OFFICES

Year End	Commercial Banks	Savings Banks	Savings & Loan Assns.	Credit Unions	Total
December 31, 1939	18,095	683	8,006	8,077	34,861
December 31, 1949	18,870	730	5,983	10,073	35,656
December 31, 1959	23,276	966	7,041	19,350	50,633

If these figures are then expressed in terms of population per office on a national basis, the following density patterns are revealed:

Table 4
POPULATION PER OFFICE

	Banks Only	Including S & L's	Including Credit Unions
December 31, 1939	6,923	4,892	3,759
December 31, 1949	7,612	5,832	4,184
December 31, 1959	7,407	5,632	3,476

During the past decade the formation of new offices has exceeded population growth whereas the reverse was true during the 1940's. Important qualifications should be made, however, which lessen the actual penetration at present.

As to savings and loan associations, there are several important categories. The S & L as we know it became legally empowered under the Federal Home Loan Bank Act of 1932 and subsequent legislation, including the creation of the Federal Savings and Loan Insurance Corporation in 1934. Most S & L's now in existence represent conversion of some previously existing building and loan association. The old B & L's were chartered in nearly all the states and operated primarily as clubs, having no public office. Many of these old B & L's still exist; the remainder have been converted to S & L's, merged by an active S & L, or in some instances liquidated. At year end 1958, the total was approximately 6,900 existing S & L offices of which 1,804 were federally chartered, 2,077 were insured state chartered, and 662 were members of the Home Loan Bank system without benefit of insurance. This totals 4,553 [5] institutions, with an estimated 1,090 branches or a total of 5,643 public offices which are open on a regularly scheduled basis. This leaves an estimated minimum of some 1,200 old building and loan associations. The figure is approximate because many are dormant and reporting by the several states is uneven. They are especially prevalent in older urban areas. These nonpublic B & L's somewhat overstate the population density as previously reported; however, their importance lies in the relative ease with which they can be converted into public institutions.

In the matter of branches or new charters or conversions of B & L's the Federal Home Loan Bank Board states: "Applications are considered by the Federal Home Loan Board on the basis of all available information and in accordance with the tests provided in Section 5 (e) of the Act, particularly as to the character and responsibility of the applicant group, the need for such an institution in the community to be served, the prospects for its usefulness and success, *and whether it could be established without undue injury to properly conducted existing local thrift and home-financing institutions.*" [6] In effect, this means that expansion or conversion of savings and loans is considered against the pattern of other existing associations only rather than against the pattern of all banking institutions in the area in question.

As to credit unions, the present degree of penetration is even less meaningful than that for S & L's since the majority are run informally within the plant or office concerned. Even so they are an element in the banking market. Moreover, many of the larger ones have established full-time offices, and especially important is the more recent development of the community type which is open to the public. Chartering or opening of public offices is not generally subject to review in relation to other existing banking institutions.

As to function, both S & L's and credit unions pay out deposits on demand as a practical matter; further, both have the power to sell money orders, which provides quasi-checking account facilities for their members. Lending functions by S & L's are rather well circumscribed but those of the credit unions are limited primarily by available resources.

The point to be made in this section is not that the growth of these other types of institutions is necessarily bad or unfair but rather that they are so close in character to banks that all types should be considered jointly by the supervisory authorities and that the institutions themselves must consider the several types of institutions in any analysis of their markets.

NEW OFFICES VS. THE ECONOMY

A comparison of this type could be carried out in infinite detail but would be of little value for two reasons: first, the utilization of national aggregates cannot be the proper basis for what must be a local consideration. Second, we know too little at this stage about the true potential of a given market and it is to this that the remainder of this analysis will be devoted. The statistics in Table 5 are presented solely as background and as bench marks by which future trends can be compared.

Table 5 [7]

AGGREGATE CHANGES—BANK OFFICES AND THE ECONOMY

	Total Banking Offices	Population	Family Income	Money Supply	Gross Nat'l Product	Consumer Price Index
Per cent change 1949–1959	42%	17%	53%	29%	94%	23%

In projecting the future the Bureau of the Census makes a medium projection of 226 million people by 1975, an increase of some 46 million, or some 26 per cent over the next fifteen years. A simple division of population per banking office into this increment would indicate some 13,200 new banking offices during that period. This, of course, makes no allowance for further changes in economic conditions or for more intensive competition. All that can be indicated is that there will be a great deal of activity in the field of banking expansion and that we need much more analytical knowledge than is presently at hand.

AREA CHARACTERISTICS

The pattern of new bank and branch interest is by no means uniform. In an effort to clarify the area for investigation, several refinements have been attempted.

Few data are available on new branches or banks under such classifications as between rural or relatively isolated communities and the larger trade areas of metropolitan communities. In an effort to obtain some information in this respect, the new unit banks actually formed in 1956 [8] were surveyed through the use of the Rand McNally [9] Bank Directory and pertinent maps. Using the arbitrary definition of suburb as a community which was part of a larger trading area containing other banking centers, the number of new urban and suburban banks formed during 1956 was 48. By contrast, the number of new banks formed in rural communities was 36. Unfortunately, there is no feasible way of making a similar tabulation for branches. Unquestionably, the larger number of branch formations which took place represented what the respective bank managements considered logical extensions of their trade areas—either offensively or defensively. Further, some of the new bank formations undoubtedly obtained impetus from state laws forbidding branches in towns or townships where a bank was already operating. The one thing the survey did show was that out of a total of 834 new bank offices opened during 1956, 36 were unit banks in rural communities. The reverse inference would seem compatible with the observed condition that most new offices were located within previously banked areas.

CATEGORIES OF NEW OFFICES

The subdivisions listed here are based on observation and evident differences rather than on any available head count. Some, such as the mobile bank, are still only novelties but are nonetheless significant in marshaling the trends for subsequent deposit analysis. A major subdivision can be made between types, however—a circumstance which is becoming increasingly clear as urban-suburban complexes mature. The division pertains to offices designed to render better service to a bank's own customers (and the competition's) at major convenience points as opposed to offices which aim to capitalize on the tangible growth of new trade areas. The division cannot be absolute, to be sure, but the characteristics are evident and, as such, are useful.

The Isolated Community

The purest type is the establishment of a new branch or bank in a relatively isolated community which has no other banking facilities. The basis for relative isolation is that this new facility, once established, has a clear-cut convenience advantage over any competing facility. Further, the idea of establishing a banking facility was influenced primarily by the pre-existence of a trading center of which the facility could become an advantageous part. This is in recognition of the cardinal principle of retail banking: banking is a convenience function nearly always undertaken in conjunction with other routine errands. This principle is a major guide, and motivating influence in all the types about to be described.

For such a banking office—with a convenience dominance —the whole trade area may be considered its oyster in estimating potential. One hundred per cent of potential is never attained, of course, for in this and every other case the individuals, merchants, and manufacturers have some antecedent banking history and hence an unmeasurable degree of loyalty.

By contrast, there is a mitigating influence which is especially prevalent in the newer and better-class suburban areas. Turnover of residents is high in such areas, which means that new banking relationships are being established all the time.

One bank in one of the better-known suburban communities estimates that its entire customer roster changes approximately once every seven years.

Actual cases of this type of pure trade area facility—both unit banks and branches—will be reviewed later.

The Satellite Trading Area

The second and probably most frequent type may be called the new subtrading area facility. Again, the existence of a new convenience shopping locus is the major influence. If large enough, the subarea may attract more than one facility. Here growth is paramount but defensive action also becomes important, with each bank having to judge its own stake in the area in question. The question of who gets there first is of major importance. No one supports monopoly as a principle, but this is frequently the fact since many such areas cannot support more than one or two facilities and the supervisory authorities may have to refuse other applications even though the applying banks can demonstrate substantial business in the area in question.

Many of these subarea facilities are in shopping centers though this is by no means always the case. In any event, estimating potential is much more difficult here since the lines both of convenience and of regular shopping habits are not predetermined.

The Strategic Access Facility

The third major type of new growth office may be termed the "strategic access" facility. This differs from the second category in that the major determination is based on a market larger than any single suburban trading point. To arrive at such a location the density pattern of both presently held and potential business throughout a major trade area is analyzed and laid out on maps for easy study. On these maps are superimposed other maps indicating the major arteries of travel between the suburban areas of desirable business and the area's urban center. From these calculations a location can be determined which will provide a convenience interception point to a good percentage of these traveling customers and prospects. Such a branch is not in any particular trading area, but it is on a major traffic artery and has the all-important drive-in and parking facilities. It has been extremely successful, both offensively and defensively.

Frequently, this will be a larger type of banking facility than is the case for subtrading areas. There are, however, increasing instances of small, inexpensive facilities located at sparsely settled edges of major areas—which could be characterized as "toll bridge" or strategic access types.

New Convenience or Defensive Types of Banking Offices

The major feature of these offices is that the primary reason for their establishment is to serve existing business better. No such office is wholly defensive, of course, but the offensive aspect is more the possible capture of competitive business than the securing of a share of new growth. A possible exception to this, in part would be the branch-on-every-corner situation that exists in the corporate gold coast on the East Side of Manhattan.

The other distinguishing mark of this type of office is that it is usually located in heavily settled areas.

Examples:

Airport offices
Railroad station offices (including limited commuter offices)
Bus terminal offices
Supermarket offices
Subway offices
Department store offices
Mobile banks

Most such facilities are of the limited type, i.e., deposit and withdrawal only, although in some cases an installment loan officer may be stationed there if conditions warrant. Most all of the above facilities require full branch investigation and approval, although many states are now allowing for special categories of limited facilities, usually quite close to and frequently physically connected to the main office. These latter are specifically limited to deposit and withdrawal. However, the FDIC does not recognize such exceptions, and full branch approval must be obtained.

Many of these are new innovations of which only a few examples exist. They are signs of banking's recognition of a changing market. However, it is difficult to generalize about their economic feasibility at this stage of limited experience.

Five other categories should be cited to complete the roster. Two of these are not even banking offices, but they constitute significant elements in modern banking.

THE PARKING LOT

The first of the nonbanking office activities is the parking lot. In one given case a bank hired a marketing expert to solve a fairly typical problem. Located in a city of over 100,000, this bank was one of three with main offices in a crowded downtown section. Feeling somewhat sensitive to criticism that it was not modern, this bank was giving thought to a drive-in branch. Analysis showed that a decent location for such an office was impractical due to traffic congestion and high real estate values. However, a substantial parking lot one block from the banking nucleus was available, and proved to be a cheaper, as well as a preferable, solution in terms of customer reaction.[10] This solution may have many applications.

IN-PLANT BANKING

The second nonbanking office practice is in its infancy but shows much promise for the future. Colloquially speaking, this development is known as "in-plant" banking. In its simplest form this means the issuance of either credits to accounts or the mailing of checks to employees representing payroll disbursements for a given employer. Other refinements include the availability at the place of employment of mail deposit forms and loan applications. It does not include check cashing on the employer's premises, as this is generally construed to constitute branch banking. This whole field is new and will have to evolve through bank-employer-employee and even union co-operation. Significant starts have been made in some instances, and this is unquestionably a trend to watch.

The remaining three categories of convenience-type offices are somewhat diverse, but most interesting.

THE PURE DRIVE-IN

Most frequently there is the in-town drive-in type of office. Usually this office is completely a service institution for accounts already held. As such, its value can best be judged by the number of cars or transactions that pass through. Such a facility is frequently operated at odd hours, in relation to regular banking hours. As a minimum rule, it has been considered successful in cities as small as 20,000, provided it is a clear-cut convenience over other facilities available at the same hours.

THE DOWNTOWN BRANCH

The second of these three types is the downtown branch. Frequently, such an office is only a block or two from the main office. It may reflect a slight shift in the so-called 100 per cent location in a city or it may be created to capture a specific market, such as one large office building or the clustering of a specific trade. In any case, such a branch is based on a highly localized market which can be analyzed by the bank from its own knowledge and records. The motive for such a branch usually comes from an obvious competitive disadvantage or advantage, so that general treatment is not warranted here.

THE OUT-OF-TOWN MAIN OFFICE

The last of these convenience types is somewhat inverse. It is in its infancy but is of great importance not only in terms of deposit attainment but in terms of capital expenditure and banking prestige. This is the somewhat bold procedure of moving the main office away from the so-called 100 per cent location. There have been a few examples and quite a few instances of serious interest in such a move. Uusually the present main office is in a crowded downtown area. However, much important commercial business is concentrated there and this makes a bank loath to leave in spite of antiquated quarters. Generally speaking, the decisions split two ways: the first is that it is all-important to remain at the center in which case a drive-in or parking lot is resorted to. Second, and this usually represents area banks rather than single community institutions, the bold decision is made to leave only a convenience office downtown and to build an adequately parked showplace some distance away. A powerful influence in the latter case is convenience for important customers from the larger area, rather than just one 100 per cent location. There have been some highly successful cases of this, and as area banks become prevalent there will probably be more.

As has been indicated, there have been many changes in banking offices in the postwar period. Some have been fads, some are trends which already show signs of petering out, and others are in the ascendancy. Regardless of type, there will be more activity in this field and the question of economic feasibility becomes paramount. It is hoped that the subsequent chapters will shed some light on this problem.

III

The Banking System and its supervisory authorities

Since the end of World War II something over 6,000 branches and about 1,150 new unit banks have been added to the banking system. Beyond this, it is impossible to tell how many such projects have been considered and discarded. In addition, there is the growing problem of extensive investment in either renovated or new main offices—a factor which adds disproportionately to the amount of banking capital tied up in bricks and mortar, to say nothing of drive-in windows and walnut paneling.

There are two problems here, each of which has grown more intensive in the postwar period:

The first is possible overbanking of a territory. It would appear from the aggregate statistics that this has not yet become the case although each area must be considered individually. Even allowing for the draw off by savings and loan associations and other savings outlets, population per office is down from some 7,400 to approximately 5,600. Against this, the statistics on liquid holdings per person have climbed disproportionately. So too have bank loans, both relatively and absolutely, and so too have interest rates. As countering influences, inflation has neutralized much of these impressive gains. Further, deposits have flattened in recent years in response to a restrictive monetary policy and bank loan ratios have reached levels which allow for little further increase other than through new absolute gains in deposits. It is evidently a complex problem. The trends involved all seem to be flattening somewhat, making each new move progressively suspect in terms of its probable margin of sucess.

The second problem is the relatively higher cost of each new operation. For practical purposes, all nonpostwar banking offices are now thirty years old or older. Therefore, they are cheap and tie up little of banking's capital. Every new move at current prices disproportionately disrupts that hard-earned advantage. As a general indicator, other assets, as a percentage of total assets, have increased from 1.20 per cent in 1947 to 2.14 per cent as of December 31, 1959.[1] The major variable in other assets is bank real estate and fixtures and the change is of the order of 9.7 per cent a year, as opposed to an average annual increase of 3.4 per cent in net total assets in the same period.

These are the problems which the supervisory authorities must consider as they face today's clamor for permission to branch, permission to build a new main office, and a host of other important expenditures which represent the efforts of 14,000 banks to improve their competitive positions.

CHANGING PERSPECTIVES

Following a decade and a half (1930–1945) of almost no activity, it is evident that interest is present, risk capital is available, and competition is keen. Conversations with national and state supervisory authorities have revealed that they receive a continuing stream of inquiries concerning new branch permits and bank charters. Usually, especially in cases of branch permits, the applicants are both experienced and objective in their efforts. However, there are increasing instances of collateral motives which, although quite legal, can color the attitudes of the applicants and cause them to seek establishment of a banking office which would not be, per se, a sound banking venture. The reasons for this center in what a bank is—a gathering point for the public's money. With the investment of the necessary capital (which also can contain a goodly share of public money) a banking operation, then, has the leverage of the deposits attained to foster economic activities of its own choosing. To be sure, there is continuing supervision of such loans and other assets by the supervisory authorities. But banking is free in the sense that each bank's management makes such loans and investments and the supervisory authorities can only comment or act after such actions have been taken. Banking must be free in this fashion in order to do its job, but this ex post facto sequence makes it highly important that the motives and quality of control and management be carefully scrutinized before any new permits are granted. This qualitative analysis of ownership and management precedes and supersedes any purely economic considerations. This is seldom a question with well-established banks, but it is a matter of constant scrutiny as bank ownership (control) has become popular in recent years among people whose major interests lie elsewhere.

The legitimate, but distracting, side aspects of banking are principally as follows: (*a*) real estate promotions, (*b*) legal fees, (*c*) insurance commissions, (*d*) controllable source of financing for another business, and (*e*) directing of collateral business, e.g., security purchases and sales. Category *b* and, to a lesser extent, categories *c* and *e* are normal outgrowths of banking operation and relationships in these fields are usually negotiated via the normal avenues of salesmanship, good service, and applicable reciprocal business. Category *a* can be dangerous, especially where a branch or bank is established merely to bolster a shopping center or add prestige to a development or redevelopment. Here the problem may lie in unwise capital expansion by the bank. Category *d* is disastrous in principle even if the business in question is sound, for the bank is surrendering its objective judgment. Notable cases include tract housing, dealer-generated installment sales paper, and single corporate enterprises which receive unjustified credit. The bank failure in Ellenville, New York, was a case largely concerning one industrial enterprise.

These situations are cited not because they are too evidently prevalent on the current banking scene—they are not. Rather, they are illustrative of the forms of healthy skepticism which the supervisory authorities must maintain. This is important because such situations, if allowed to fester, can cause crises for an entire banking territory that is otherwise healthy.

"The principle of free banking was significantly modified by the Act of 1935 which provided that, in addition to capital requirements, certain other factors needed to be considered if an overbanked condition was to be avoided." [2]

Prior to the depression banking was a free enterprise system in which capital could be risked in the hope of profitable returns. There was regulation then and there is even more stringent regulation today. It is still true that banking is a private enterprise in that capital may be risked with the expectation of a future return. However, the criteria for allowing the running of such a risk have changed, in recognition of the larger economic consequences of endangering public moneys. For this reason a stricter criterion of public need has come to the fore in considering new branch and bank permits. In addition to public need there must be, of course, evidences of capable and honest management, sound ownership, and intention to operate the privilege of a banking location in a proper manner.

THE DUAL SYSTEM—HISTORY

The standards of judgment in banking have come slowly and, under a democratic lawmaking process, only after painful experience. It would be useful to review that experience briefly.

The United States started its career without a meaningful banking system. Foreign currency—notably British paper money and Spanish gold dollars—was the principal medium of exchange. In 1791 the First Bank of the United States was founded under the leadership of Alexander Hamilton. Hamilton believed in a strong central government and a strong central bank. This first bank had a rather brief life during which it made some attempts at providing a stable currency. The ultimate value then as now was gold, and the ultimate realization of value was the ability to redeem in gold whatever currency one held. What few banks there were found it quite profitable to issue their own currency—redeemable in gold. Their prosperity, however, lay in avoiding such redemption since this would naturally curtail the scope of their operations. The central bank tried to police these other banks by presenting such currency promptly and demanding gold in payment. But the abhorrence of strong central control in government which early Americans shared with Thomas Jefferson was reflected in the attitude of the independent banks. The combination legislated the First Bank of the United States out of existence in 1811.

An important but little remembered fact here is that the Constitution, reflecting the fear of a strong central government, prohibited the issuance of paper money by the federal government—which forced reliance on banks of issue of some type.

Following the extinction of the First Bank, local banks under state charter (the only type available) mushroomed and so did inflation, especially following the War of 1812. By 1816 the central forces prevailed, and the Second Bank of the United States was created. It lasted until 1836 during which time it was a good but hated and little understood watchdog of the currency-issuing habits of state banks. The latter part of its existence was highlighted by a running controversy with President Andrew Jackson. The bank made many mistakes in the years of conflict which only added to the popular belief that it was an evil monopoly of the moneyed aristocracy. Its death in 1836 was hailed as a great triumph for Jackson and the little people.

From that point until the Civil War, American banking succeeded more or less in spite of itself in the midst of violent physical growth. The wildcat banks howled in the wilderness and the United States Treasury was reduced to running its own cashbox, so to speak, as there were few banks it could trust to safeguard federal moneys. The re-establishment of a central bank, however, was politically unthinkable.

Central banking has two major functions, monetary control and serving the needs of the federal government. The second need became overwhelming during the Civil War, and the next major steps in banking evolution took place. First, Congress authorized the issuance of currency directly by the government, the greenbacks. Second, favorable legislation was enacted to allow the creation of, or the conversion of existing state banks into, national banks. A central bank was still politically unthinkable, but a degree of uniform supervision was attainable by making it most attractive for banks to convert to national charters.[3] Many did, especially the more important banks, for the law gave them the advantage of being able to issue currency against collateral of government bonds as well as against gold. This, incidentally, was a major aid in the placement of the federal debt created by the Civil War.

Following the war both national and state banks grew and reasonably good currency stability pertained. Because of easier standards, state banking again became predominant in the early twentieth century, passing national banks in deposits held, having passed them in numbers in the 1890's.

Financial panics occurred fairly regularly in the late nineteenth century and came to something of a climax in the panic of 1907–1908. These panics convinced many knowledgeable people that the banking system was unsafe because there was no place for banks to turn to in periods of temporary distress.

The result was the Federal Reserve System, enacted in 1913, which provided a point of central help to deserving banks—subject, of course, to many qualifications and safeguards. The Federal Reserve Act itself was a compromise and a concession to the still strong desire for local autonomy—twelve regional banks were created rather than one. As further compromise to these sentiments, state and national banks were allowed to retain their previous identities and supervisory systems. As a final and major compromise, membership in the System was not compulsory.

Possibly even more important for the discussion at hand, the currency-issuing function was taken away from private banks and placed with the Federal Reserve Banks.

This left the two systems at something of a standoff. Federal Reserve membership developed slowly, and the two separate systems were perpetuated. National banks generally were subject to more severe supervisory scrutiny, not in terms of relative laxness but in terms of permissible functions. This was (and is) true especially in the field of mortgage lending, as well as in several other functions. Against this the prestige of a national bank was substantially higher, especially in rural areas and in other locations where the public had firsthand memories of bank failures. Numerically, such failures were far greater among state than national banks. Conversely, state bank capital requirements were usually somewhat less stringent than national regulations, and new state banks were thus more easily founded.

The depression temporarily brought down the entire banking system; Federal Reserve members fared best and state bank nonmembers fared worst—especially small rural institutions. The reforms of the Banking Acts of 1933 and 1935 are well known and again, from the point of view of the issue at hand, independent pressure resulted in a legislative standoff in so far as national versus state banks were concerned. The effort to make Federal Reserve membership compulsory for all banks subscribing to the new Federal Deposit Insurance System was narrowly defeated. A significant portion of state banks (in terms of assets held) then joined the Federal Reserve System.

However, there are still more state banks outside of the Federal Reserve System than there are members. Statistics as of year-end 1959 showed 6,885 nonmember state banks as opposed to 4,542 national banks and 1,687 member state banks.[4] From the point of view of the desirability of unified supervision, this continuance of the dual system is somewhat lamentable. However, in fairness it must be said that most states have set their regulations so that they largely parallel national requirements. The National Banking System has a strong sense of pride, as do the state banks and their supervisory authorities. Although Federal Reserve membership includes the overwhelming majority of bank assets, it does not, as shown, have a majority in numbers. Federal Reserve has control over monetary policy, but it has not replaced the dual system in bank supervision. This latter, of course, includes decisions on bank charters and branches.

This entire discussion of the development of the dual system has one major relevance here. Permission to operate a banking location carries with it unique advantages in that the chances of a second institution being given permission to operate in the same area are substantially limited by the criteria of economic feasibility. Under a dual system, there is competition for representation in such localities from both sides, and occasionally the "firstest with the mostest" principle can cause one set of supervisory authorities to act with

less than complete objectivity. Conversely, one set of authorities may approve a merger in which the surviving institution
as a single entity has been deemed adequate to serve the
needs of a given community. Against this, the opposing supervisory authority may authorize a new branch or bank on the
basis that the community in question needs another banking
institution.

To compound the problem further there is dual—federal
and state—authority over similar moves by savings and loan
associations. The federal supervision is completely separate
from the banking system, whereas the state authority is frequently the same department which has responsibility over
state banks.

As with the earlier-mentioned problems of possible overbanking and overinvestment in real estate, these are not meaningful or flagrant problems at present. They are on the ho-
rizon, however, as possible factors in an era of intensive competition.

Before going on to the actual organization of the supervisory authorities, it should be said that excellent standards
have been set by all supervisory parties and that, indeed,
healthy competition has been fostered in many instances by
the existence of the dual system.

Banking Activity—Present Circumstances

Of the fifty states fourteen have practical prohibition against
branches in any form.[5] In the other states branching privileges
vary from home office city to state-wide with the most frequent situations being limitation to home office county or
contiguous counties. In all instances state legislation determines this, and the National Banking System conforms to the
existing situation within each state. Notable extremes are the
state-wide privileges in California, Connecticut, and others as
compared with the prohibition in Illinois, Texas, and Florida,
among others. There is steadily increasing pressure for greater

branching privileges in many states, and the recently enacted "Omnibus Bill" in New York State could be highly significant in this respect.

It is not surprising that the larger states prohibiting branches have seen the greatest formation of new unit banks. However, thirty-four states approved one or more banks during 1956 and the pattern has touched nearly all the states since the war.[6] Supervisory authorities are of the opinion that this category of interest will continue to grow, even in the presence of unlimited branching privileges. All states have enabling legislation for the possible formation of new banks.

As for savings and loan associations, there are both federal and state charters available in this field. Federal charters and branching permits are under the authority and supervision of the Federal Home Loan Bank Board in Washington. State charters and branching permits are under the supervision of various state authorities [7]—usually the same authority that supervises state banks. The pattern here is mixed, however, with federally chartered associations operating relatively autonomously and with the criteria for state associations frequently not in conformity with state bank criteria. The present and probable future importance of these associations indicates some further legislation to achieve more uniform supervision. Here, too, the desire for independence will fight a strong battle, and for practical purposes the savings and loan field is not included in the subsequent discussion of supervisory authorities.

There are three major areas of activity with which the supervisory authorities have to contend: (1) the desire for new banking offices, (2) the virtues of mergers, and (3) the attitude of the public in respect to both. Generally speaking, the public does not object to new banking offices nor indeed to mergers except that local identities may be lost thereby. What the public does object to is anything that to them appears to smack of monopoly or, even more important, anything that appears to be big and powerful and somehow too much for the individual to strike a fair bargain with. These fears hark back to Andrew Jackson and are sure to be fanned in any legislative attempts to enlarge existing state banking laws. Public concern is an ill-defined thing and is more a matter of reaction to personal exposure than to any real understanding of or genuine concern with changes in the structure of banking. As such, it is more a responsibility of banking itself than of the supervisory authorities.

With this atmosphere of public interest, or rather hopeful absence of public antagonism, decisions must be reached on the two major trends—physical expansion and organizational merger. It must be borne in mind that both types of action come only on the initiative of the bank or banks concerned. They create the situation which the supervisory authorities can either approve or disapprove.

THE DUAL SYSTEM—SUPERVISION

There are two places to go in search of permission to open a bank, to open a branch, to effect a merger, or indeed to close a branch or bank. For institutions seeking such permission under the National Banking System, the place is the Office of the Comptroller of the Currency in Washington. For such permission under state charter the place is the Department of Banking and Insurance (or similar title) in the state capital in question. In addition, such moves will also be subject to approval by the Federal Reserve System and the Federal Deposit Insurance Corporation if the involved organization is or hopes to be a member of these institutions. The first two, however, represent the central authorities under the dual system.

National Authorities

The Office of the Comptroller of the Currency has the responsibility of granting charters for new national banks throughout the country. This office is a division of the Treasury Department. Other than granting new charters, the Comptroller supervises currency issuance, existing national banks and branches, and several other functions assigned by the Treasury Department. Physically the Comptroller's Office and staff are located in Washington, D.C. Field supervision, for national banks, is effected through District National Bank Examiners located in the headquarters city of each of the twelve Federal Reserve Districts. These Chief National Bank Examiners in each district are the people who investigate and screen applications for new banks and branches under the National System. Final decisions rest with the Comptroller with heavy reliance upon the reports received from the District Examiners. The Comptroller's authority in the matters of national charters and branch permits has been well defined by law and court review; it is not, in specific cases, subject to review in the courts.[8]

An interview with a National Bank Examiner brought forth the following criteria in evaluating a new bank charter or branch permit:

1. Does the area need a bank?
2. Can the area support a bank?
3. Is the management capable?

Background information forms used in applying for a national bank charter or branch permit are included in Appendices I and II. The economic aspects will be discussed in the several case studies. The important thing is that the burden of proof is on the applicants.

Operation under a national charter requires membership in both the Federal Reserve System and the Federal Deposit Insurance Corporation. Each of these institutions has its own examining group, and they usually work in concert with the national authorities in considering a new situation.

State Banking Authorities

Each state has a banking department under various titles. This department has the power to grant new bank charters and branch permits as well as related duties, principally the supervision of existing state banks, building and loan associations, and insurance companies. Requirements sought by such authorities usually parallel those required by the national banking authorities. There are significant variations, however, and an attempt has been made to generalize them citing legal sources. This summary is included as Appendix III.

Options for State Banks

As a further consideration, the state bank has the option of operating as a member of both the Federal Deposit Insurance Corporation and the Federal Reserve System. Membership in the Insurance Corporation may be had singly, but membership in the Reserve System requires the Insurance affiliation. It is useful to point out certain advantages and disadvantages in each of these affiliations.

FDIC vs. Non-FDIC

(pro) 1. *Public prestige.* Interest in deposit insurance is probably the area of greatest critical inquiry on the part of the banking public. As such, its acceptance is almost universal among banks—as of December 31, 1959, some 372 banks with assets of approximately $2 billion were not insured as compared with 13,625 banks holding assets of $284 billion in the insured category.[9]

(con) 2. *Insurance premiums.* Although there is some dissatisfaction with the method of assessment, which includes frequently overstated year-end figures, insurance premiums are considered a cheap price to pay for this important element of prestige and protection.

(con) 3. *Extra examinations.* This is always a task for all concerned. However, FDIC examiners work in concert with other examining authorities to minimize the load. For the 6,000-plus state banks which are not members of the Reserve System, FDIC examinations are a necessary burden to their choice of membership and from an over-all viewpoint are highly useful in that they provide the largest single area of uniform supervision within the banking system.

Federal Reserve vs. Nonfederal

(con) 1. *Increased number of reports necessary under membership.* While burdensome to prepare and of little use to the individual bank, the collation of weekly figures from reporting member banks has been a major factor in bringing monetary policy to its present level. The practice has come full circle, in that banks now rely heavily on these figures in their own portfolio planning.

(con) 2. *Additional examinations.* As in the case of FDIC membership, this is an extra burden which the several sets of authorities are trying to minimize where practicable. In addition, however, there has been evidence that the Federal Reserve Banks are injecting new conceptual aspects into their examination criticisms, viz., that too large a portion of bank loans are in the term category. These are in the realm of enforcing monetary value judgments via examining authority. It is not in this purview to debate them except to say that from the viewpoint of the member bank they are an element of restraint.

(con) 3. *Interference with state and national supervisory positions.* For national banks this is not a usual problem in that Reserve membership usually involves standards approximating those of national banks in such matters as type of loan and degree of margin, interlocking directorates, capital requirements, permissible investments, and other banking operations. For state banks, however, these same requirements of membership represent somewhat more stringent regulation (see Appendix III).

(con) 4. *Increased cash needs due to reserve requirements.* There are four aspects to this objection: (1) membership requires that reserves be carried in the District Federal Reserve Bank, (2) balances with correspondent banks do not count, (3) vault cash does not count as part of required reserves,* (4) nonmember reserve requirements are lower or less precisely computed under many state laws. Each of these justifies some amplification. Membership entails the maintenance at the Federal Reserve Bank of specified percentages of both demand and time deposits. Such figures must be computed daily, and the average requirement must be achieved on a cumulative basis twice a month. These must be net deposits at Federal Reserve representing money collected according to the Federal Reserve availability schedule, i.e., float or uncollected items do not count. The importance of these requirements will be evident in the discussion of the three remaining points.

Before going into this discussion it should be pointed out that Federal Reserve provides real service in the collection of checks on a uniform availability schedule. With the exception of some few nonpar points (small banks which charge a fee for paying for their own checks when presented), Federal Reserve will pay the collecting bank good reserve money for a check on any bank in the United States two business days after presentation. In many instances, Federal Reserve does not get actual reimbursement that quickly, and as a consequence is actually extending free credit to the extent of the difference. This is the well-publicized float that usually rises in the middle of each month, which is the period of most active collection. This granting of two-day availability would be an overwhelming reason for Federal Reserve membership if it were not available to nonmembers. However, it is available through the simple medium of sending checks to a cor-

* This has recently been removed.

respondent bank which is a member. Only because of this does the remainder of this particular discussion have validity.

Balances with correspondent banks do count as reserves for nonmembers. As nonmembers, such banks can keep proportionately handsome accounts with their correspondents and expect, and get, an astounding roster of services in return. To be sure, Federal Reserve performs many correspondent services, particularly in the fields of check and draft collection and security safekeeping, which are also provided by the correspondent banks. However, there is no incentive reward aspect to this type of activity by Federal Reserve, whereas competition is keen among the correspondent banks. Member banks use the System largely as a necessity in the heavy physical services because they cannot afford the duplicating compensating balances which correspondents would need to perform these services. Member banks are, therefore, penalized in that they are forced by economic pressure to use Federal Reserve's services and what balances they do keep with private correspondents must come from what would otherwise be earning assets.

The matter of vault cash has now been solved by legislative action and Federal Reserve has until 1962 to allow such holdings as part of required reserves. This will remove what has been a distinct penalty on members, especially national banks, which could escape this disparity only by surrendering their national charters. This latter has been the case in many merger situations and after many years of debate this thorn is being eliminated.

While too lengthy to enumerate here, it can be generalized that reserve requirements for state nonmembers are nowhere higher than Federal Reserve requirements and in several states are lower (see Reserves in Appendix III). More important, most nonmembers compute their reserves by adding together all their cash and due from bank items. This can include items mailed to correspondents that day for collection two or more business days later. Since most such banks do not need to calculate the dollar value of deferred items, they have a continuing advantage to the extent of their outstanding uncollected items.

(con) 5. *Higher capital requirements.* Again the various state requirements are too numerous to list here and are of interest to particular parties only for their own state. For this see sections "Capital and Surplus" and "Branch Banking" in Appendix III for further references. See also the Hoffman thesis on "Bank Chartering Procedures" listed in the bibliography.

Some useful summary guides can be provided by comparing the national bank requirements for capital for new banks with the summary compiled in 1954 by the State Bank Division of the American Bankers Association as part of their report on "State Bank Supervision." This is confidential, but permission has been obtained to reproduce their summary tables on capital requirements.

Initial capital funds must be broken down into three categories: capital, paid-in surplus, and reserves for organization or possibly some other descriptive term covering moneys which will probably be spent during organization.

Table 6

STATE BANKS—CAPITAL REQUIREMENTS

Minimum Capital Required *	Number of States Reporting 1954 Survey
No Minimum	1
$10,000	1
15,000	3
20,000	1
25,000	27
35,000	2
50,000	12
100,000	1

* 37 states have statutory surplus requirements, usually a per cent of capital. All states expect some surplus and/or reserves to be paid in over and above the capital itself.

National requirements are, of course, uniform and are scaled to population. Nearly all states also scale to population to varying degrees.

In further inquiry, the survey found that nineteen of the states felt their minimums should be raised and that as a practical matter amounts higher than the minimum were already required in most cases. The ABA State Legislative Committee, in its model bank chartering statute, suggests the minimum requirements given in Table 7.

Table 7

SUGGESTED STATE STANDARDS—
AMERICAN BANKERS ASSOCIATION

Population of City	Minimum Capital
3,000 or less	$25,000
3,000–6,000	50,000
6,000–50,000	100,000
over 50,000	200,000

Comparatively, national bank requirements are as given in Table 8.[10]

Table 8

CAPITAL REQUIREMENTS—NATIONAL BANKS

Population of City	Minimum Capital *
under 6,000	$50,000
6,000–50,000	100,000
over 50,000	200,000

(except as stated below)
In an outlying district of a city with a population exceeding 50,000 provided state law permits organization or state banks in such locations of $100,000 or less.

* Plus cash surplus of 20%.

The third element of organization reserves (also known as undivided profits) varies widely. It is actually a terminological recognition of necessary expenditures rather than a separate fund. In all states surplus and these other funds are expected to provide the cushion for organization expenses and the inevitable losses of early operation.

Almost universally state authorities have the right to set capital requirements above statutory minimums and the tendency has been to exceed such minimums. National standards have been adhered to rather closely, except in occasional large bank formations. As an example, of the 120 new banks chartered during 1956, only 14 had capital of less than $100,000.[11] In recent years this point of difference between the two sides of the dual system has narrowed substantially, with actual requirements approximating national requirements in most instances.

Higher Capital Requirements—Branches

The best single statement that can be made here is that capital requirements for branches are comparable to those for new unit banks. This means that each applying branch must examine its present position as to capital adequacy in relation to its present offices and on a pro forma basis to include the additional requirements which the proposed branch would bring in.

(pro) 6. *Assured borrowing facilities*. This feature was central in the creation of the Federal Reserve Act as the element designed to avoid temporary banking crises. Such crises of a purely banking type have largely been avoided since 1913, but not directly because of the rediscount window at the Federal Reserve Banks. Rather, the psychology of its presence and the maintenance of continually adjusted reserves have brought about this condition of elasticity—stability—within the banking system. In fact, as banks learned in 1921 and again in 1930–1931, the requirements and standards of borrowing eligibility are entirely too strict to be of much help to a bank in trouble. This is probably as the Federal Reserve

System wants it to be, because an automatically open window would be conducive to lax banking practice. These tenets were stanchly reaffirmed in the November, 1959, bulletin of the Federal Reserve Bank of New York. In spite of its relative disuse, this is one of the Federal Reserve's most important aspects. Nonmembers exist in the belief that either they will not need such facilities or that they can count on private correspondents for such facilities. This latter was indeed the case for many institutions during the thirties and remains the basis for strong relationships. It is a question each bank has to weigh for itself, but it is evident that the larger banks of the country have decided that they could ill afford to rely on another private institution against a time when both would probably be in difficulty.

(pro) 7. *Prestige.* This factor must be considered at two levels which are related to the markets served by the banks in question. The public does not seem to be aware of membership as a prestige factor to any meaningful degree. Certainly not to the extent of FDIC membership, and this is reflected in the relative emphasis on the two in bank advertising. The second level is that of banks which hope to obtain business from corporations and other knowledgeable institutions. In these instances it is recognized that a nonmember comes in for a bit of extra scrutiny, but there does not appear to be any prejudice provided the bank's ratios are in line and its management well commented upon.

(pro) 8. *Support of federal monetary policy.* Probably the most important reason for membership is also the most elusive in terms of direct benefit to the individual member. It is rather like being put on a leash which may be alternately tightened or loosened. This may be disputed in two opposing ways. First, Federal Reserve's policies as to reserve requirements are followed by state authorities, changes in rediscount rates are followed by private lenders, and Federal Reserve influences spread throughout the open market so that nonmembers are subject to monetary control in any event. Oppositely, a bank can believe in the usefulness of federal monetary action and get its "benefit" without being a member. The answer lies in effective control, which the Reserve System unquestionably enjoys and which most bankers believe it must have to avoid monetary chaos.

In sum, the presence of active correspondent banks mitigates much of the need for membership—especially for smaller banks—and as nonmembers such banks enjoy certain definite competitive advantages. The Federal Reserve control in terms of dollar assets in membership as opposed to those outside is overwhelming so that the situation is not a problem. It is and should be a matter of continued scrutiny and accomplished changes, such as the vault cash reserve allowance, in order that the gap not become too wide. Today, as in 1836, it is politically unlikely that the public would accept a single national banking system, so probably the dual system will continue—with some benefits and some inequities.

Considering the various reasons for affiliation with the several groups described, it is interesting to note that of the 1,050 new banks chartered from 1946 through 1957, 926 obtained insurance, 203 were national banks, 85 became state bank members of the Federal Reserve System, and 638 were state nonmembers.[12]

Movements among existing banks are less easy to tabulate, new insurance memberships progress steadily, but little change occurs in other affiliations except through merger. Banks do not take such steps lightly.

Lastly, there is the human element in contact with the supervisory authorities. In general this represents a high level of civil servant, well versed in his field, and striving at all times to be judiciously fair in what is almost always a matter of economic conflict between two or more institutions.

The best presentation in approaching these people is a frank and honest one, sobered as much as possible by an objective appraisal of the situation at hand. In the case of branches, if the motive is largely defense of existing business—display it;

if the motive is to capture an as yet unfeasible locality—justify it with sound future projections. New unit banks do not have this leverage in either form and can only lead from the strength of a quality organization group and a sound economic prognosis.

This is stressed only because the competitive byplay is bound to get more severe as time goes on. There is a selling aspect to it, of course, and the group which makes the best presentation should, ipso facto, have the best chance of succeeding in its proposed venture.

IV

Measuring deposit potential

In actuality no move in terms of a new banking office can be considered as a pure case. Even if the office is to be established in a relatively isolated community with no other facilities available, there is a competitive consideration to the extent that there is existing banking business from the community which, perforce, must be lodged elsewhere. In the true sense new business means accounts from individuals and organizations which had no banking accounts before. As such, new business is not likely to be as attractive as old business and old business must come from some other institution or institutions.

Therefore, all considerations of new banking facilities have two sides: the positive demonstration of economic need for and ability to support a new facility and a negative demonstration of the probable absence of undue competitive injury to existing institutions. Supervisory requirements for economic data in support of each application are such that, if properly prepared, they will demonstrate the positive side while providing information so that the authorities can properly judge the negative aspect. It is the purpose of this chapter to outline such requirements and to make some suggestions as to their proper presentation.

Before doing so it is highly important to define certain salient circumstances, the definition of which will help to provide a more objective focus within which to work. First, all such efforts at banking expansion are an effort to capture additional retail business for the institution in question. So-called wholesale business is not to be had on the basis of establishing a new office. All such business has a banking history with loyalties and dislikes and various degrees of established opinion as to banking practices. In wholesale business the mountain goes to Mohammed in the form of bank officer calls and other types of cultivation. Such accounts are comparatively few in number and large in relative importance, and they exist in a quid pro quo which is defined in larger terms than pure convenience of a teller's window. This is not to say that a given bank will not have a better opportunity to share in the wholesale business of a community because of a banking location there. It will eventually, provided a good new business job is done. This takes time, however, and should not be included in any initial estimates unless firm and specific commitments are at hand—the individual categories of deposits will cover this more fully.

It follows, then, that what is being considered is retail business; and more importantly, that retail business is more a function of convenience than of any other positive factor. Indeed, a decided advantage of convenience can offset such negative factors as higher rates, austerity of personal contact, and sloppy bookkeeping. The reverse is not usually true, however; a crackerjack institution cannot overcome the penalty of a poor location.

Thus, having defined our criterion, there remains only the definition of the commodity which such analysis seeks to estimate. The commodity that is the subject of this study is deposits. Deposits are the base material of banking without which the rest of the operation is meaningless. Conversion of deposits into earning assets has been the subject of much written work and is subject to much more precise calculation than the subject at hand. This is true because the common denominator is known and the results are a matter of policy application and algebraic expression. Although there will be illustrations of assets and earnings in the cases that we shall examine, they are either actual or hypothetical and based on averages. Investigation of markets for loans and investments is not appropriate here. Two overwhelming reasons why the asset side is less subject to generalized analysis are: (1) the wide variation in banking policy as to asset application and (2) the fact that the market for loans and investments is nationwide if not world-wide. People will walk a great deal farther to borrow money than they will to deposit it. This latter fact has implications, too, for retail borrowing markets as opposed to retail deposit markets.

BACKGROUND DATA

Charter applications require, as supporting evidence, a financial history of the community in question together with the location and description of other financial institutions within a specified radius. Such applications also require pro forma or projected statements for the new facility covering at least two years of operation. Preparation of these data presume a thorough analysis of the market. As previously mentioned, it is always easy to be overoptimistic and the quality of the supporting evidence can play a major role.

There are listed below the major economic factors required in support of a charter application. These factors were extracted from the questionnaire required for a national bank or national bank branch application. The full questionnaire is included in Appendices I and II. Requirements of state authorities are generally similar.

1. Population of town and population of trade area (with maps).
2. Wealth characteristics: home ownership, income, commercial trade volume, manufacturing sales and payrolls, seasonal characteristics and long-range outlook (this is a broad category and the quality of the answer is most important).
3. Financial status of the town: assessed valuation, revenues, collections, and debt.
4. Competitive institutions and their locations (with maps).
5. Financial history of town and its financial institutions.
6. Demonstrated need for a new banking facility.
7. Estimated competitive impact.
8. Projected or pro forma statements for the new facility.

A great deal is required here; some of it may not seem to be directly or measurably pertinent to actual deposit potential. However, at minimum, both sides achieve a more rounded picture through its gathering and it is therefore useful. The work involves three stages: defining the area, gathering the raw data within the area, and translating the data into actual potential.

The Trade Area

The concern is with retail business, which is the convenience business more favorably available to a given location than to some other location. The assumption that retail business is a convenience business is further narrowed down by many analysts of banking situations as follows: retail banking involving visits to the bank is a side aspect of convenience shopping, i.e., groceries, mail, drugs, and other frequently performed purchases. The inference is that the location must be attractive because of other features which draw the individual to the area and that banking must follow this locus of points. There is a further inference that a shopping locus of a more specialized nature, e.g., department stores, specialty shops, and other less frequent major purchase types, will not draw banking customers from a more accessible corner-store type of grouping. To a large extent both of these inferences are true although there are two discernible categories: work convenience and travel convenience, which run somewhat counter and will be considered. With these exceptions, the retail trade convenience principle will determine the trade area. In fact, the role of branch banking is to recognize this aspect of human economic behavior.

Knowledgeable human instinct of those who have worked or lived in an area can usually supply the definition of a trade area in its major elements. However, that same instinct nearly always suffers from habit, which sometimes causes faulty vision. Therefore, it is important to use some testing methods to verify local knowledge. This is especially true of more recent trends which have yet to reach full force.

A trading area is determined by customers and their habits. These habits—shopping patterns and traffic flow—are then retranslated in terms of a geographic area. There have been many refinements within the concept of a trading area—such subdivisions as primary and secondary, 50 per cent of customer concentration, etc. It is strongly suggested that any such secondary or peripheral areas be not considered in realistic planning. The only possible exception would be the fact that the other centers which cause the questionable determination have no banking facilities. This again is the type of variable which an intelligent survey would disclose.

Almost entirely this study is concerned with the determination of a new trading area for a new facility. A related type of analysis is that of the trading area of an existing bank or branch. This bank has the huge benefit of being able to pattern the location and characteristics of existing customers. This is a technique of growing interest in relation to new main office locations and so-called defensive types of moves, and in some cases the strategic access type of branch. The emphasis here is on a new primary type of trading area.

In analyzing such an area, there are two basic questions:

1. What are the existing patterns of traffic flow and shopping habits which define this area in relation to the proposed bank office location?
2. To what extent will future trends, such as new highways or growth of other new nearby centers, affect this trading area?

These future trends should include the influence of the new bank itself as its presence will unquestionably have some bearing on these shifting patterns.

Trade area analysis has usually employed three aspects of a plotting of travel time between the proposed bank and the areas considered to be possible components of the trade area. These three with comments are as follows:

1. Development of a pattern based upon an arbitrary trip of, say, ten minutes by automobile. By itself this method suffers from the fact that it is arbitrary—convenience in a thickly settled suburban region is quite a different concept from that in more far-flung areas. This analysis does have the virtue of providing one aspect of the trading area. It will reveal greater "reach" along good roads as well as the effects of physical barriers, such as mountains, railroad tracks, rivers, etc.
2. The second method is a break-even line around the location based on equal travel time between the proposed bank and its competitor's location or locations. Again, this method gives only an abstract expression of customer choice based on a choice between banking facilities with no consideration of other influences. It will provide a useful second map to supplement the study.
3. Study of shopping patterns and actual traffic flow. This is the empirical approach, which shows what people are doing for whatever reasons affect their choice. Whatever the reasons, this method ties in with the assumption that retail banking is a convenience purchase type

of transaction. Assistance in shopping-pattern development can sometimes be obtained from merchants who
will allow location sampling of their customer records.
With some of the larger chains, similar analysis is standard practice and occasionally available. Street-inter-
ception interviews can be helpful if brief and well handled, as can sample telephone surveys.

Traffic flow is a complementary but less clear-cut tool since
it includes through traffic and lacks definition of intent. Nonetheless, a fourth map showing relative use of the several access
roads should provide further refinement.

Positive Valence

In addition to, and following, these three steps there is a relatively simple method for more firmly establishing the boundaries of a primary trading area. The three steps and four
maps already cited should have a great deal in common. Also
they may show areas of variation or create unclear impres-
sions concerning certain sections. It is proposed that these
indefinite areas all around the suggested periphery be sub-
jected to sampling interviews at home and in person. The
samples need not be large and bank personnel can be used.
By asking a few simple questions the direction of people's
convenience shopping habits can be ascertained. There are
pitfalls here and refinement of the questions by trial and error
may be necessary. It is important to keep the interviewee on
the subject and to avoid value judgments. For this reason
many pollsters suggest leaving banking out of the interview
entirely. The subject can become very complex [1] but it is believed that a few brief questions consistently applied will
bring forth consistent samples. The question at hand is an
indication of dominant consumer purchase habits for the questionable outer limits of a trade area. The bank should be severe
in its interpretation of these samples. Since the areas under

investigation are already somewhat in doubt, anything less than, say, 75 per cent positive response should be ruled out.

It is believed that this sampling as a follow-up to the first three steps will provide a boundary to the area of positive valence for a given location. Some business will be obtained from beyond these boundaries, to be sure, but it is not predictable enough to be included. In the process of going through these four stages, the bank will learn much about its proposed market and, on the basis of the convenience shopping premise, can establish a well-founded area of positive attraction which may now be called the trade area.

TYPES OF CASES

At this point it would be useful to reiterate the discernible types of cases together with any generally pertinent comments on trade area definition which apply to each.

Isolated Community

This is the easiest type of community to define whether it has an existing banking facility or not. It may well include some fairly distant and scattered sections which the positive valence technique should reveal. An existing institution could, by sampling its records, know this even better than a new survey. However, when such information is not available, the survey must be made independently, more or less along the lines just described.

Where a new branch is being considered, it may be that the bank in question would already have significant business in the area. If this is so and there is no present banking facility in that area, a plotting of this business indicates the degree to which such a move may be defensively important. On the other hand, if there is already a facility at the location under consideration, an analysis of existing business may be most revealing of the true trading area for that location. Such analysis may indicate that a location other than the presumed center holds greater potential. Unexpected results of this type are not infrequent and well justify the expense of trade area analysis for existing banks.

In general, however, the isolated community situation is one in which the location is assumed based on established habits. This is a must for new unit banks and frequently so for branches under the criterion of demonstrated need. It also presumes that most of the effort is in terms of new business, although defensive situations must be considered. From the extreme of the isolated, nonbanked community, all cases grade downward with increasing emphasis on the defensive.

New Suburban Areas

The principal difference between this situation and the isolated community is that the lines are more blurred. Habits may be in a state of flux and future trends need to be carefully interpreted. Often a new shopping center gives rise to this type of situation. If so, the positive valence must be checked as firmly as possible, since the margin may be quite small. This analysis is more difficult because probable future habits are being studied, rather than established ones.

Suburban sites which have developed a focal point more gradually than a shopping center have the benefit of some degree of established habits to draw on. This can work both ways, however, in any trade area. Foreseeable changes through either natural economic change or planned change, such as new highways or municipal developments, must be considered. A trading area does not remain constant and it can decline as well as grow. Sometimes a large specific activity can change the pattern abruptly. Not the least frequent is yet another shopping center which would drain a large segment of the considered trading area.

The defensive problem crops up frequently here and at minimum each bank should have current knowledge of the geographic distribution of its customers. Rapid decisions are often required, and it is important that most of the homework be done in advance.

Strategic Access Positions

The one clear-cut aspect of this category is that it would be extremely difficult to justify a new unit bank at such a location. A strategic access location can be defined as a point on a well-traveled artery, but a point which is not the center of any trade area nor even necessarily adjacent to any store group. Such locations usually emerge from an analysis of existing customers and of the growth statistics of the several smaller subareas in which they are located. The principal reason for such an office is defensive—to render better service to existing customers—but it has decided offensive aspects too, especially if the convenience proves attractive to competitors' customers similarly distributed. A brief but most informative description of one such analysis was published in *Banking* magazine and is well worth reading as a unit.[2] Much of the procedure employed is integral in this discussion as described in the strategic access case.

With the growth of smaller shopping centers and residential groupings, together with increasing local branch-type competition, access-type branches may become more important. Establishment of a branch, even the simplest, represents a substantial capital outlay which will be of concern both to bank management and to the supervisory authorities. If, as suggested, the competitive tenor becomes more acute, the strategic access branch may frequently be the solution to serving several smaller convenience areas, none of which individually justify a branch.

Established Trading Areas

The two major aspects of new facilities in established areas are: (1) they are primarily defensive (other than new unit banks) and (2) the location is not prejudged but is usually the result of customer analysis and trade area analysis. Frequently this becomes the strategic access type of situation within a fully settled section. As such it can vary from a full branch bank to the limited facility which consists of only a drive-in window. The main reason for differentiation is that this type of facility results from a re-examination of an older area already served by the bank in question and probably one or more competitors. It can also be the base for a successful new unit bank as Case G will illustrate (page 89).

Another change within established trade areas that is gaining increasing interest is main office location and facilities. In a few instances analysis of the trade area of existing customers has led banks to build new main offices at some distance from the supposed trade center. Usually this is the result of realization that the majority of customers are located so that the trade center has only incidental meaning to them. This is especially true of area banks rather than single community institutions.

Where the reverse is true, banks have made efforts to make their location in the trade center more accessible. This can be accomplished through renovation, drive-ins, better parking, and in some cases through the simple expedient of establishing a separate parking lot within walking distance of the location. It is difficult to generalize about these latter moves and it is equally difficult to estimate the success of the more purely defensive types of facilities. Utilization is the main indicator, and the record of a limited facility (drive-in deposit only) will be described as Case D (page 83). All of these are reactions to trade area analysis and are subsequent efforts to better the service of existing business as well as to capture new business. Substantial money is at stake in each such move and trade area analysis is an inexpensive and essential preliminary thereto.

BASIC SOURCE MATERIALS

Once a trade area has been defined, it is then necessary to number and evaluate its contents. There are three general categories of source material: published data, surveys by other interested institutions, and direct investigation by the bank.

Published Data

The primary source of vital statistics, of course, is the U.S. Census. However, this can be frustrating in many respects since the collected data may not provide breakdowns directly related to the trade area in question. As an aid, a compilation of what the various census reports do provide has been made and is included as Appendix IV. For new suburban and for rural areas the survey unit is liable to be too large for the purpose at hand. In the more populous areas, census tracts, if available, are ideal because they contain quite complete and chronologically consistent reporting on small well-defined areas. Generally speaking, however, the more useful information comes from other sources in which experts have used census figures as the basis for more refined and updated data. Chappell's article on bank use of census data [3] is well worth reading if direct recourse to the census is considered necessary.[4] Frequently reports published at the state level are more directly useful, and usually are published by the State Department of Commerce. A trip to the local public library will reveal many such sources, including city directories, municipal planning studies, etc.

One extremely helpful source is the *Survey of Buying Power* published yearly by Sales Management, Inc., of New York. Although its primary focus is on retail trade volume by community for other types of stores, it must be remembered that a bank is a store too. These surveys report population and income for quite small communities and are almost always useful. Possibly these figures on spendable income are more realistic than census income figures, since the latter suffer from the well-known underreporting bias.

Another useful published source is the municipal *Credit Survey* published yearly by Dun & Bradstreet, Inc., New York. This provides current information on ratables and other vital statistics on municipal entities with outstanding indebtedness of $500,000 or more. There are many others with varying degrees of usefulness which will be uncovered in the course of inquiry.

Surveys by Other Interested Institutions

More often than not the best data are near at hand, having been compiled by another institution with a strong interest in local retail activity. Utility companies are especially helpful in this respect as they have a stake in measuring future growth. Others include public transportation companies, supermarket chains, and the several levels of local government. School boards are especially helpful as they are concerned in depth with the relatively small school districts and will have good information on population as related to pupils. A start at local inquiry will usually set off a chain of sources which will help fill out the portfolio of local statistics.

Direct Investigation

From the bank's point of view, direct investigation is the best way to verify the raw data for the trade area in question. This need not be expensive and can usually be done by sampling in respect to some variables whereas a complete count can be made on others. The key is to divide the proposed trade area into small subareas which are as homogeneous as possible. Once this has been done, a complete count of dwellings can be made. Sampling can then reveal the probable population based on average number per family. Sampling plus previously available information should provide a good generalization of per family income. Actual counts are easy in terms of commercial and industrial activity with the aid of Dun & Bradstreet's regular credit reference book. Any investigation which has been pursued to this point will probably have turned up other local sources of information which will further document the case.

The Important Variables

At this point it is time to enumerate the variables that are truly useful in subsequent deposit analysis. It is all too easy to accumulate a wide variety of statistics which will be of little value. The key variables to be determined are population in terms of family or spending units and the income levels of those spending units. In terms of individual retail business these are the only ones that really count. It is necessary to refine them by considering other characteristics of those spending units, such as average age, ethnic homogeneity, and type of occupation. These other characteristics can provide a definite correlation in terms of average balances in relation to income. All the other variables, such as house values, per cent of telephone or television installations, cars per family, etc., are derivative of the two keys—numbers and incomes—in the same way as are bank balances. Concentration in these areas will provide the basic raw data.

DEPOSIT POTENTIAL

The question may well arise as to which should be determined first, the location which determines the trade area or the area which provides the potential. This is a chicken-and-egg kind of dilemma. However, the two investigations complement each other and will provide their own resolution. This resolution can only follow successful conversion of the raw data into deposit potential. One obvious method is by comparison of the area in question with the actual achievements in other comparable areas. To some extent this is possible with isolated areas or with suburban sections. However, to be possible, comparability must be assured by the enumeration previously described. A random listing of deposits attained in one bank town by population categories was plotted on a scatter diagram. No meaningful trend line could be obtained and it is evident that numbers alone do not ensure comparability. However, potential estimates can usefully be correlated to similar situations if comparability as to income characteristics has been obtained. This is an excellent way to provide a fix on an otherwise independently obtained estimate but can be used only as a cross check and then only against three or more other situations.

For example, an estimate of $5 million is probably sound if the mean of three other situations is, say, $4.5 million. Actual attainment is always less than true potential and the important thing is that comparability estimates show consistency. Such comparisons can be gathered by using the Rand McNally Bank Directory and some income reporting service such as the *Survey of Buying Power.*

The original estimate, however, must be done in depth by direct consideration of the market at hand.

Analysis of Market by Type of Deposit

Inductive analysis of a defined market is a new and relatively uncertain field of statistical correlation. Actually there is available only one set of survey statistics which apply in this field. These surveys are being continued and further improvement is expected. The surveys in question are the joint effort of the Federal Reserve's Board of Governors and the Survey Research Center of the University of Michigan. Entitled *Survey of Consumer Finances,* these studies are an attempt by sampling to develop representative data on consumer assets and debts by income class and other pertinent variables. The latest available survey was published in three parts in the March, June, and August, 1957, *Federal Reserve Bulletin* and is reproduced as Appendix V.

Utilizing that portion of the *Consumer Finance Studies* covering checking and savings accounts [5] and other experience gained in the preparation of this book, it is suggested that the deposit potential of a given market can be estimated in four categories as follows: Individual Accounts, Commercial Accounts, Industrial Accounts, and Public Moneys.

Individual Deposit Potentials

Analysis must be based on comparable data by subareas, which means areas in which the wealth characteristics of the population are similar. Assuming that such delineation of the market has been accomplished, it is possible to translate this market into dollars of estimated deposit potential. Survey results as to the average deposit potential per family by income bracket were reported in Tables 9 and 13 of the June, 1957, *Bulletin*, pages 571–572. These tables are of the incidence-within-brackets type of statistical reporting, i.e., 8 per cent of all spending units with incomes $5,000 and over carry no checking accounts, 28 per cent have average balances in the $1–$499 range, etc. These data were converted into over-all averages by income bracket as shown in Table 9.

Table 9

DEPOSIT POTENTIAL PER FAMILY [6]

	Family Income		
Average Balance	Under $3,000	$3,000 $5,000	Over $5,000
Savings	$360	$480	$880
Commercial	190	270	590

These data are the potential per family in the area and allow for the fact that many families carry no account. These are nation-wide averages and consideration must be given to other characteristics of the population. Older people tend to exceed these averages, whereas younger people will be below average. Regionally, the Northeast has higher averages than the rest of the country. First- and second-generation immigrant areas tend to yield higher averages in savings and lower checking account averages. Also, the data on savings accounts include postal savings, shares in savings and loan associations and credit unions, in addition to savings accounts in commercial and savings banks. There are a number of reasons why these very general statistics should not be used without refinement based on local investigation. Indeed, specific experiences have varied so widely from these general averages that many experienced bankers consider them valueless. The cases which will be discussed illustrate this and Chapter VI is devoted exclusively to suggested ways in which a given institution can better appraise its own situation. Since the overwhelming portion of the potential for any new banking office lies in these categories of individual demand and savings accounts, this area deserves primary attention in market appraisal. Consequently, the foregoing figures are presented only as a brief generalization which has been based on limited sampling.

Commercial Deposits

This category includes the various merchants and professional practices which are located within the proposed bank's anticipated trade area. They should be listed individually by name and if possible interviewed. There is no generalized formula to be followed here. Stores which are parts of larger chains will have their banking policies dictated from outside. In some of these instances decision on a bank is automatic and based on convenience only. In any event, inquiry of the store manager and corporate treasurer will give a rather good idea of the prospects and average balance.

In the case of locally owned enterprises, each must be considered as an individual case. Each was in business before the proposed bank and therefore each has a banking history. The only way to learn their intentions is by interview.

In the average new bank situation the organizers can cover this field without too much difficulty. Initial enthusiasm should be treated with great skepticism, however, as people are poor estimators and also are generally loath to move banking accounts.

Once the field has been canvassed, the firms should be rated as to financial size by use of Dun & Bradstreet Listings.[7] These ratings should then be used as a means of comparison with the average of other enterprises in that field and financial bracket.[8] The purpose of this is to obtain average cash figures for the industry as a correlative check on the estimates given in individual interviews.

The individual interview not only is the one known reliable method of estimating deposit potential but its great virtue is that it forces a more realistic determination of the bank's probable trade area.

Industrial Deposits

The only way properly to estimate the industrial deposit potential within a new bank's market is by individual investigation. Aside from convenience in the encashment of payroll checks, industrial companies tend to bank for reasons other than convenience. This is especially true of larger multiplant companies, whose moneys tend to be concentrated in large centers. Further, there are wide variations by industry and by the financial status of each concern which render averages rather meaningless. Since the normal new bank's market will contain relatively few industrial enterprises, the only realistic approach is by individual investigation.

Public Moneys

The nature of this category indicates the need for individual investigation. Major fields are federal, municipal, and state deposits, together with the several governmental agencies such as school boards, parking authorities, etc. Each trade area is unique in this respect, and the bank's organizers should be able to conduct the necessary investigations. There is occasionally a case of "too much" in this field if the organizers represent concentrated strength in one political party. Subsequent elections could cause drastic adjustments.

Actual vs. Potential

As may be gleaned from the foregoing, the critical emphasis should be on individual deposit potentials. In this respect it must be admitted that the average deposit potentials previously cited constitute statistical heresy and were presented only as a preliminary guide. The full tables on type and size of selected liquid asset holdings within income groups are included in Appendix V. The reason why averages are misleading is inherent in the nature of the reported data. For example, the reporting showed that in the $6,000–$7,499 income group 30 per cent had no checking accounts while 37 per cent had checking accounts ranging from $1 to $199. This kind of information is the result of sampling experience which has shown less distortion than other possibilities, such as estimating averages. However, it is folly to lump the 30 per cent and 37 per cent as 67 per cent having checking accounts of arbitrarily, say, $100. Further, it is self-deception to assume that the 37 per cent which had checking accounts of $1–$199 should be averaged as $100 per spending unit within this group. More probably, if the individual data were available, those persons reporting checking accounts within this range would report a median balance of, say, $120 and a possible average of $135. These comments should be illustrative of the fact that each area under investigation is worthy of scrutiny beyond mere averages. This becomes increasingly true in the higher income brackets. For example, in the same $6,000–$7,499 income bracket 7 per cent have checking accounts ranging from $500 to $999. An assumption that this means 7 per cent of people within these income brackets have average balances of $750 would probably be an understatement of the pure statistical reporting as obtained.

There is the question of accuracy of sampling in the statistics presented here and there is also the problem of reliability in the gathering of such sensitively personal information. As the Federal Reserve has strongly pointed out and as history at the end of many financial panics has shown, people will either hide or underestimate their liquid holdings. All of which is to say that, although the Federal Reserve statistics are the only general data available (and they do provide a consistent plot of year to year change), they are suspect of general understatement and even as provided must be treated with proper statistical reverence.

CAUTION

The foregoing is generally bullish as to potential estimates. It must now, and most sharply, be brought out that the biggest single weakness in this whole business of estimates is the actual share of business that a bank can expect to attain. Irrespective of the quality of the analysis of potential, the actual penetration of a new banking facility is a matter of guesswork and ex post facto generalization. Many factors are at play here: policy, aggressiveness, location, and the actions of competitive institutions. It is impossible to generalize on these matters, but recorded history can provide some clues. It is for these reasons that the subsequent case studies are presented.

V

New branch cases[1]

THE NEW SHOPPING CENTER CASE

Bank A is a commercial bank of $24 million deposits that contemplated opening a branch in a new shopping center on the fringe of an eastern city of some 85,000 population. Because of the mountainous terrain, the surrounding communities (with another 65,000 in population) made up the maximum possible trade area for this center. Both area and city were quite old and were dominated by moderately heavy industries with pronounced cyclical characteristics. Population was in a gradual declining trend, the city's downtown section was extremely congested, and the whole area had more than enough banking facilities.

Total area deposits were $120 million at year-end 1958, of which $52 million were demand, $28 million were commercial bank savings, and $33 million were savings and loan shares. Thus roughly half of all deposits were savings and a bit less than half of these were lodged in commercial banks. The eleven commercial banks had nineteen offices, and the eleven savings associations had fourteen. Figures are not available for the relative growth of S & L and bank savings.

Income distribution throughout the area was relatively uniform, and the market survey prepared for Bank A by an outside consultant estimated median family income at $4,300. The income level in the city itself was slightly higher.

A puzzle immediately arises in estimating the probable savings level per family. If the national averages from the *Survey of Consumer Finances* are used as a guide, the savings level of this income range is $400–$500 per family, with an additional $250–$300 in checking accounts. These figures, of course, make allowance for some nonsavers. On the other hand, if total area savings of $61 million are divided by the number of families, a savings level of $1,470 per family is indicated. Apparently, without examining whether banks and savings associations had other than local, individual depositors, the surveyor picked the larger figure for use in his projections. His very plausible reasoning was that savings are known to be proportionately higher in older, industrialized eastern communities with fully assimilated minorities.

The shopping center location was urged upon Bank A as a means of drawing business from the congested downtown areas. The center, well located and tenanted by good names, was the only one in the entire region and, from the bank's viewpoint, was distant from competition, with one negligible exception. Annual sales of the center were estimated at $8 million. Total area personal income was roughly $180 million, supposedly more than ample to support such a center.

The surveyor was quite conservative in his projection of potential depositors. The trade area for personal deposits was drawn to include only those districts which lay within a mile radius of the center and which, furthermore, were not already served by a bank. It seems obvious, of course, that the ultimate penetration of this banking location should reach beyond such narrowly set limits.

In the trade area so defined lived 5,800 families with income of $27 million. The surveyor eliminated 25 per cent of these as being present customers of Bank A and projected that 25 per cent of the remainder could be expected to save at the shopping center branch. This is equal to 1,100 families having average income of $4,770 and estimated savings of $1,470 each. The total savings deposit potential for the branch was thus $1.6 million, a target which should be achieved in a few years.

As for commercial deposits, the surveyor assumed that only the businesses at the center would use the branch. He made no provision for municipal or industrial business. Total demand deposits, including individual checking accounts, were set at a potential $750,000 including deposits transferred from other offices of the same bank.

Actual Attainment

After permission was granted by state banking authorities, the branch opened in mid-December, 1959. The figures below summarize performance to date, as well as anticipated potential:

	Demand	Time
June 30	$146,000	$ 72,000
September 30	166,000	90,000
Potential	750,000	1,600,000

The 260 savings accounts had an indicated average balance of roughly $400 at the end of September.

Hypothetical Comparison

The question, of course, is why savings have so far failed to measure up to expectation. The following hypotheses are offered:

1.   Family savings, though higher than the national average in many industrialized communities, are likewise forced down

by recurring unemployment in areas (such as the one described here) dominated by cyclical heavy industry.[2] Since the average savings balance so far is actually only $400, not $1,470, this factor probably should be given some weight. Re-evaluating deposit potential, then, in terms of, say $500 per family, the target for the defined trade area becomes $550,000 rather than $1.6 million.

2. An unexpected recession began early in 1960 and has since intensified, striking industrial areas such as this with rising unemployment. Not only are promotional efforts made more difficult, but it is likely that families would not care to transfer savings balances that are being drawn down, partly out of pride and loyalty and partly from a desire to maintain whatever credit standing may have been established.

Aside from unemployment and recession factors, Bank A serves a stable community, with little or no in-migration and possibly very low housing turnover. Assuming that banking is a convenience, a kind of family habit such as buying a loaf of bread, this sort of residential stability might very well freeze banking loyalties more than we would expect in growing, fluid communities. In other words, the customary survey practice of marking out 25 per cent of a trade area as fair game should probably be re-examined, with adjustments made up or down depending on the mobility of the population. This could be roughly measured, for instance, by school registrations or utilities billing records.

New business promotion, of course, is the crux of success in establishing a new banking office. Where deposits expectations are not being met, promotional techniques should be carefully examined among the other factors discussed above. Branch A apparently has an uphill fight.

THE SAVINGS INSTITUTION CASE

Bank B is a savings bank in an old settled community of some 32,000 population—a community which has long been the central trading point for a much larger surrounding area. Town B is a seaport and the sea is a major factor in its economic life. In more recent years it has attracted, in addition to a sizable naval facility, several industries, and a growing summer population which is not included in the population figure just cited.

Town B is, as cited, old and its downtown area is highly congested. The town supports three commercial banks with deposits estimated at $50 million, a $20 million savings and loan association, and the savings bank in question with deposits of some $55 million. In the aggregate, these holdings of some $125 million are well in excess of the national average and indicate the older savings-minded community which Town B appears to be.

In recent years Town B and its environs have enjoyed good growth due to the influx of new industry both military and civilian. Wishing to capitalize on this new growth, Savings Bank B applied for a branch in a new shopping center. Town B's over-all trading area is sharply delineated by the river on which the town is located. This is a large river and access, within the area, is limited to a toll bridge just north of the town over which passes the major highway indicated on the map. The shopping center was formed facing this highway and within one mile of the bridge on Town B's side. Savings Bank B applied for a branch in this shopping center and employed an outside consultant to prepare an economic brief. This brief will be summarized here and then followed by a hypothetical comparison and comments, together with the actual attainment of the branch which has been open for about one and one-half years.

Economic Considerations

The survey considered the five townships shown on the accompanying map as the probable trade area for the branch in question. The drawoff of deposits in Town B and by the banks in the town across the river were mentioned and con-

THE SAVINGS INSTITUTION CASE

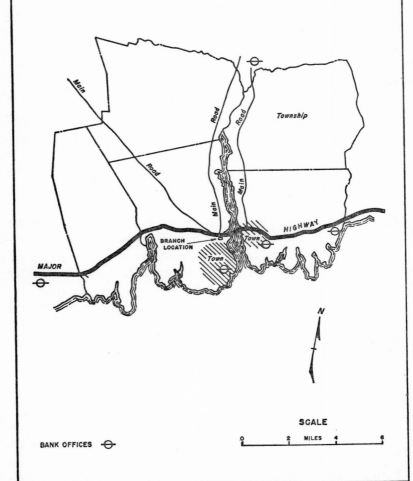

MAJOR

BANK OFFICES ⊖

SCALE

0   2   MILES   4   6

sidered in the following survey (summarized) which was the basis for the application.

A major point was made regarding the character of the 25 stores in the center as to their drawing power—especially a large Sears, Roebuck, which was the anchor of the shopping center. This supposed drawing power was the justification for including all five townships plus Town B in the estimates of trading area potential.

The survey reported an estimated 1957 population of 85,000 for the entire area—the figure being updated from the 1950 census via State Department of Health figures. Other statistics included new dwelling units constructed, a 1950 census breakdown of certain sections of the population by occupation, and a generalization (justified) of probable future growth.

The survey estimated 3.5 persons per family or some 24,000 families within the area. Reference was then made to *Sales Management,* which in 1956 estimated after-tax income of $6,600 for the town and $6,300 for the county.

This survey dealt in aggregates and the preceding information led to the conclusions that the 24,000 families had pretax incomes of $7,000, or a total income of $170 million per year. There was then some recital of retail trade in Town B gleaned from the *Census of Retail Trade.* Total sales figures for Town B and County B were quoted from *Sales Management.* There followed an estimate of $10 million as the annual sales volumes of the shopping center in question.

The survey then turned to the *Survey of Consumer Finances* and proceeded to estimate the savings potential for the five-township area. In this case the incidence-within-brackets method was used with the range of balances in each bracket being settled at the arbitrary halfway point: viz., 13 per cent of families in the $5,000–$7,499 income bracket save from 20 to 29 per cent of their income; this was translated as 13 per cent of the total area families multiplied by 25 per cent of their estimated average incomes of $7,000. This expression resulted in an estimate of total annual savings of $23 million for the whole area.

The survey then went on to make the point that cumulative savings were far more important than those of any given year and estimated the five-year cumulative for the area in question at $135 million.

The survey then stated its assumption that one third of this total, or some $39 million, would be placed in savings accounts—the rest going into insurance, mutual funds, house equities, etc. As a further refinement, the Federal Reserve Board table "Type and Size of Liquid Asset Holdings within Income Groups" was cited to demonstrate savings account balances per family by income group. Following the procedure previously used, an estimate of $26 million was achieved for the proposed trading area. After sundry comments on the drawing power of shopping centers, the survey concluded the potential for the proposed shopping center branch as follows:

First Year	$ 650,000
Second Year	1,100,000
Third Year	1,700,000
Fourth Year	2,600,000
Fifth Year	3,500,000

Hypothetical Comparison

Issue is to be taken with this survey on several points. First, the trade area seems completely unrealistic, especially in view of the admitted existence of a shopping center with both commercial and savings bank facilities along the highway in the town just east of the toll bridge. Since savings rates were competitive, this would seem to eliminate much of the area east of the river on a positive valence basis. Second, the method of the survey is somewhat suspect in that it cites total statistics for an arbitrary area based on political boundary lines. Third, there is no correlation or explanation of the total statistics of the area in relation to the subsequent estimates of potential for the branch in question. Granted, the per cent penetration by a proposed new office is the biggest element of guesswork in this whole business; nevertheless, it is absurd to leap from a mass of aggregate statistics to a final estimate without some statement, even if it is the admission of an educated guess.

To reconstruct, it would appear that the positive valence area contains most of the three townships west of the river, together with more sparsely settled areas to the north and west. Further, it is admitted that positive valence in terms of savings banking only is less well known since presumably many of the people in the income brackets being considered will also have checking accounts. Indeed, reference to the "Type and Size of Selected Liquid Asset Holdings within Income Groups" shows that 73 per cent of all families will have checking accounts. Further, and for the same reason, it is not justified to include all of the population of thickly settled Township B (which includes Town B) in the aggregate potential. There may well be some competitive penetration in this area, and a transferral of accounts from main office would be an indication of this.

The population of the three townships on the west side of the river approximates 25,000, to which may be added the more proximate 10,000 (one-third) of Town B plus another 5,000 of more scattered population to the north and west. This gives a total of 40,000 or, at the rate of 3.8 people per family, a total of 10,050 families. The 3.8 rate is used as being more representative of the younger population in these areas.

Reverting to the same table on savings account holdings, these families, on the basis of an average pretax income of $7,000, would indicate total savings of $9.7 million in savings accounts. At this point the big guess comes into play. Savings accounts are considered to be less mobile than checking accounts; further, many of the families in the area are both young and new to the area. Opposing this, the families cited are all within a fairly clear-cut positive valence area for the location in question and their newness should direct them to the branch in question. Further, the area is growing rapidly—and this is a decided plus.

Based on the foregoing and considering the single-function nature of a savings bank, a conservative estimate would be that this branch could capture 30–40 per cent of the positive valence market barring the appearance on the scene of other banking institutions. This would mean some $3–$4 million without allowance for further growth of the area.

Actual Attainment and Prospects

Attained deposits at the end of two months were $252,000. During the course of the first full year of operation customer desires were explored and $500,000 of accounts were transferred from the main office. Total attainment after fourteen months was $1,450,000, of which $950,000 was new business generated by this office. During the first full year of operation 1,260 accounts were opened, representing an average balance of some $550 per account.

Average balances are lower than the over-all average statistics, indicating the preponderance of younger, newly migrated families. Penetration based on numbers of accounts including transferees is about 20 per cent of the estimated families in the trade area. In this a slight allowance has been made for the fact that some families carry more than one account. For a new situation and a new shopping center, the early penetration has been excellent and bodes well for the future.

The professional survey is under the mark even if no consideration is given to transferred accounts. The nub, of course, is in estimating the per cent of total potential that will be attained. In this case early penetration has been excellent, but average balances are well below either average or median for the supposed income brackets. This is only further indication that such figures are at best preliminary guides and corroboration from other sources must be sought in using them.

THE STRATEGIC ACCESS CASE

Bank C was a fifty-year-old institution in a well-established farming center. As of year-end 1959, it had deposits of $7 million, $3 million of which had been achieved since 1955. The area was growing rapidly due to new residential development, successful farming, and the immigration of desirable industry. At the same dates, 1955 and 1959, its rival across the street had deposits of $6 million and $8 million. Bank C in recent years had been the more aggressive and now wished to capitalize on the present and future growth of the surrounding area. Although still predominantly the trading center for a rural area, Bank C and Town C were experiencing strong growth of retail and industrial types. They were fourteen miles from a major manufacturing city which in itself was part of a highly industrialized belt of which Town C was increasingly becoming a part. A major turnpike passed just east of the town and a major commercial highway passed just to the west.

The principal area of growth was to the west-southwest of the town partly as the peripheral expansion of the city some fourteen miles away and partly from locally generated activity as the surrounding land area had been found attractive by several industries.

The downtown section was typical—old and crowded, with little in the way of parking facilities. Both banks occupied characteristic dwellings—stone with vaulted ceilings and with no opportunity for drive-in or parking facilities.

Bank C prepared its own economic research in support of the branch application. In doing so it was guided by two major factors: (1) the law of the state in question gave branching permission to only one institution within a given township and (2) their own observations of the direction of greatest growth.

The state law in question is somewhat unfortunate as can be seen from the map on page 77. Too much emphasis is placed on arbitrary boundaries; a branch or unit anywhere within the township pre-empted the entire township from any further bank locations except new unit banks which could justify themselves on the basis of economic need. In this case the township entirely surrounds the town and the township, although not thickly settled, is divided artificially by two main highways. Bank C prepared its economic brief on the basis of township statistics rather than on statistics of the probable trade area, which contains only the western part of the township but also includes the other areas to the northwest and southwest of the proposed location. Bank C's economic instincts, however, were at work in choosing their proposed branch site.

The site qualifies under the definition of a strategic access location, since its location was based on traffic flow past an important checkpoint rather than on being the center of a shopping nucleus. Indeed, there is nothing on the location except a gasoline station at the intersection corner, with the bank to its west. The intention of the location, which has ample parking and drive-in facilities, was to capture business which was new to the probable trade area as well as to give better service to Bank C's business and its competitor's business in the almost 180-degree section west of the major highway.

With this background, it is interesting to consider the bank's own estimates and attainments against hypothetical comparisons based on an assumption of the trade area. Based on a superficial examination, a trade area of positive valence passing by this location is indicated by the dotted lines on the map. This area is all to the west of the major highway since people on the east are not likely to make the difficult crossing to do their banking business as a function separate from other shopping.

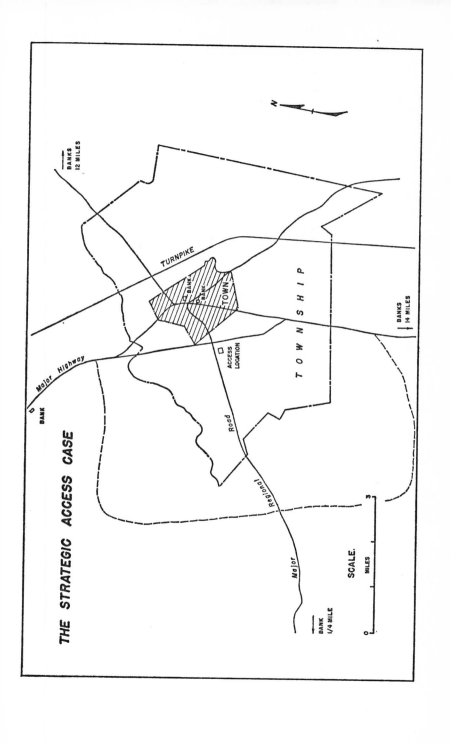

THE STRATEGIC ACCESS CASE

Bank C's Projection

Bank C cited a land area for the township of over fifteen square miles. The 1960 census reported a population of 1,280 and an extrapolation by township officials based on 1957 voting registrations gave an estimate for that year of 2,200 persons. Also cited to illustrate growth were a yearly charting of new construction, school board estimates of future need, and the existence of some 6,000 acres of good land available for development.

County Abstract indicated a true value of real and personal property of $23 million and an average 96 per cent current tax collection during the past five years.

Also cited were four new industrial plants with an estimated employment of 1,200. All these plants were located in open country to the west on the regional road where the branch site was proposed. Nearest competition as cited on the map consisted of the bank across the street in town and a bank four miles to the north and one six miles to the west on the same regional road.

Bank C dwelt at some length on the automobile banking facilities which the proposed branch would provide and which were unavailable in Town C because of limited space. This was an implied but not documented commentary on the defensive servicing of existing business by the proposed branch.

The estimated population of 2,200 was assumed to represent 630 families, and reference to *Sales Management* showed average family income after taxes of $7,600. Bank C then referred to the Federal Reserve Board's "Survey of Consumer Finances" and estimated total time and demand potential at $1.5 million from these families. To this Bank C added an estimated potential of $1 million from industrial, farmer, and municipal sources. The bank estimated a first-year attainment of 10 per cent of this, or $250,000.

Estimated Earnings and Expenses

The proposed branch was to be approximately 15 x 30 feet on slab construction with one drive-in window and three inside windows, plus platform space for two desks. The breakdown of projected earnings and expenses was concisely done and is reproduced here, as both the format and itemization should be of interest.

Table 10

PROJECTED EARNINGS AND EXPENSES—
STRATEGIC ACCESS CASE

Cost:	Land	$ 13,000	
	Building & Development	40,000	
	Machinery & Equipment	7,000	
		$ 60,000	
Expenses:	Tax and Insurance	1,000	
	Salaries	4,000	
	Light-heat, etc.	1,200	
	3% interest on nonearning assets	1,800	
	Building and maintenance	1,000	
	Miscellaneous (transportation, stationery, etc.)	2,000	
		$ 11,000	
Estimated Income: Deposits at the end of first year		$250,000	
	Estimated return allowing for reserves and float—3%	7,500	
	Loss		$3,500
	Deposits at end of second year	$500,000	
	Estimated return allowing for reserves and float—3%	15,000	
	Profit		$4,000

Hypothetical Comparison

As previously mentioned, the branch projection considered the entire township in arriving at its deposit potential. This is certainly erroneous in relation to that portion east of the limited access highway and probably also erroneous in relation to most of the center of the township, which lies east of the major highway. The probable trade area based on the access concept would include the western third plus areas indicated within the dotted line in other adjacent townships which would appear to be positive valence areas to Town C and would pass the access point in their routine travels.

This area also approximates fifteen square miles but enjoys a slightly higher population density than the township. Based on interrogation and available maps the area in question probably contained 750 families at the time of branch opening. Family income statistics throughout the area would be reasonably uniform at about $7,600 after taxes. There are no retail trade centers in the area other than an occasional small store.

The population, other than a few large farmers, is primarily young, family raising, employed in manufacturing, and owners of homes averaging five years of age. The age and relative financial burdens of this group would bring their liquid asset holdings somewhat below the national average for the same income brackets. Observing this but also allowing for underreporting, it is estimated that the average holdings in savings accounts for this type of family would be some $1,100, whereas the average checking account balance would be around $400. There is much developed guesswork in this plus some corroborative comparing with other situations. Further, it is recognized that the per cent penetration of the proposed branch would probably be higher in checking account than in savings account business. Considering these factors and allowing for a modest amount of commercial business and of municipal funds, the following hypothetical attainment is suggested after a period of two years:

Demand—60% of potential		
.60 x 750 x $400	=	$180,000
Savings—40% of potential		
.40 x 750 x $1,100	=	330,000
Commercial		40,000
Municipal (75% of township)		50,000
		$600,000

Actual Attainment and Comments

After eighteen months of operation the strategic access branch had some 362 savings accounts totaling $290,000, or an average account of $829. This is all new business opened at the branch. The numerical penetration was good and if some recognition is given to the existence of more than one account per family the average balance is also very satisfactory.

In the demand category Branch C had attained $250,000 in 480 accounts for an average of $520. To consider properly the retail aspects of this, three commercial accounts of $40,000, $20,000 and $15,000 should be treated separately. Taking these out, the remaining accounts represented an average of $366. Here again penetration and average appear to be good. The commercial business is important also, for one of the accounts is new and the other two definitely enlarged by the improved service which location C provides.

Another favorable aspect of attainment here is the report of income and expenses after one year. Branch C had income on new deposits of $13,200 for the year and expenses of $13,700. Both compare favorably with the bank's projections. The low level of operating expenses is keyed to salaries, which results from part-time supervision and one full-time teller at the start. In sum this is an excellent case of intelligent planning by a small bank with results that bode well for the future.

THE LIMITED SERVICE FACILITY

This type of branch is gaining in popularity especially with banks whose main offices are in crowded downtown locations with no parking or drive-in facilities. In many states, if the branch is near the main office and offers only deposit and check-cashing facilities, the normal criteria of demonstrated need are waived. However, the FDIC usually calls for a full report (see Appendix IX). The purpose of such a branch is one of better convenience service to existing customers rather than an attempt to capture the new business of a newly growing area. Nonetheless, there is the hope that such a limited facility, strategically placed, will attract competitively held business and as such be a growth factor.

The major difficulty with limited service facilities is in measuring their value to the bank. Unlike the consideration of new offices in growth areas, facilities of this type are usually the result of a recognition of need for better service to existing customers. As such they are defensive measures and their value is primarily a defensive one. No separate records are kept in such instances nor are accounts assigned to them in regular practice. Consequently, the only means of measuring the relative success of such facilities is an item count of physical transactions. As a generalization, bankers have not achieved any unanimity as to what degree of activity signifies a successful limited facility. The only way really to know the value of such an installation is to discontinue it—an unlikely event.

The Sample Case

This case was chosen because the bank in question feels that its limited service facility has been a successful venture. Bank D has two branches in other towns as well as its main office and limited facility in Town D. Town D is the county seat of a large farming county which is also undergoing rapid residential growth in one quadrant somewhat removed from Town D. Population of Town D approximates 9,000 but a much larger area is served in terms of banking business. Bank D has approximately $20 million of deposits which are assigned to the main office and are serviced jointly by the main office and the limited facility. The main office is located on a downtown corner and is accessible only by foot traffic. The limited facility is two blocks away and has been in business for about three years. It has three drive-in windows and two walk-up windows plus limited parking facilities. The service facility is open from 8:00 A.M. until 6:00 P.M. one evening a week. The main office and its competition are open from 9:00 until 3:00 and from 6:00 to 8:30 on the same evening.

The activity of this facility was surveyed for a twenty-workingday month with the following result:

Checks Cashed	9,176
Deposits to Demand Accounts	6,740
Installment Loan Payments	1,248
Money Orders Sold	640
Savings A/C Deposits	1,352
Christmas Club Deposits	1,444
Mortgage Payments	224

This is an aggregate of 21,824 transactions in the month surveyed, or some 218 per window per day. As a generalization the drive-in windows were more active than the walk-ups especially in the deposit transactions. Loan payments and money orders tend to gravitate to the walk-up windows. The president of Bank D estimates this total as approximately 40 per cent of the total nonmail traffic for the two offices in Town D. In view of this degree of utilization the limited facility is considered a worthwhile venture even though there is no known way of estimating its value. Perhaps the best measure is that of number of visits as compared to the older office which a limited facility is designed to supplement. On this basis Bank D would appear to have a successful limited facility.

VI

Negative branch cases

THE NO-ROOM-FOR-THREE CASE

Proposed Branch E is a useful case because it is a frequent type of situation in today's banking picture. The bank in question is an institution of some $175 million with ten offices, five in the home city and five in neighboring communities. Proposed Branch E concerned a town some 14 miles distant which seemed to hold promise and from which the bank already held some worthwhile business. Town E was already served by one commercial branch and one savings institution.

Background

Township E is a large and attractive one. Its principal industry is farming but the majority of its population commutes to work in one of two cities, some eight and twelve miles distant. Population in 1950 was 4,800 and probable present (1959) population projected from school enrollment data was estimated at 9,600, or 2,800 families. Future growth is expected at a fairly steady 500 people per year. Location is such that a geometric mushrooming of population is not likely. Median income per family is estimated at about $7,300. This compares favorably with the two nearby cities, which have medians of some $6,150 but is understandable in view of Township E's commuter status. From this, income for banking purposes is estimated at $20 million. This latter correlates favorably with an assessed valuation of $47 million—the usual situation being somewhere between two and three times income for an area without any significant manufacturing facilities.

Commercially, there are about 100 enterprises, 65 of which are within the central shopping area. None is of a large or specialized nature.

There were 15 manufacturing companies of which four were of fairly large size. Total employment was around 500 workers. One of the larger companies already maintained its main banking business with the inquiring bank.

Present Banking Facilities

The commercial branch already in E has been there some six years and has a modest, attractive location in a small but apparently successful shopping center. Its success in deposits was not known but could probably be placed somewhere in the $2-$3 million range. The inquiring bank enjoyed some $850,000 of deposit business in E at the time of investigation; of this slightly under $800,000 was in regular demand deposits, $27,000 in special checking accounts, and about $50,000 in savings. The inquiring bank had felt little competitive loss to the established branch except the drying up of trust business leads over the past six years.

The savings institution was an old, well-established one with adequate but modest facilities. Its deposit attainment (recent rate 3½ per cent) was $11.2 million or an average per account of $2,170, which is in line with the larger area.

Conclusions

An urban-rural area of this nature can, on the basis of available statistics, support a commercial banking facility as well as a savings facility. The total statistics—population of around 10,000 and total income of some $20 million—are on the low side for usual metropolitan branch consideration but possibly adequate for a more rural community. However, this town is already supporting such facilities and it would appear that the existing commercial branch has enjoyed only limited success. Further, a rough computation on savings potential would indicate some $5,000 per family in savings deposits, including savings banks, and savings and loan associations. On the basis of 2,800 families this potential would approximate $14 million, of which the local savings institution already has slightly over $11 million.

Although demand deposit business is less easily calculable, a similar condition would probably be found (consider the $800,000 already held by the inquiring bank). Town E leaves little to be tapped by a new branch.

THE UNDERDEVELOPED COMMUNITY CASE

Proposed Branch F is useful as an illustration of a growing area, the calculated potential of which was deemed inadequate for the near future. The bank in question was fairly typical: some $14 million in deposits, with only one office serving a rather fully settled upper-middle income suburban area. The bank was desirous of growth and looked at Township F, which was contiguous, as a possible branch location. Township F is a worthwhile example of the Johnny-come-lately school of post-Korean War suburban expansion. It is a fairly large land area, not directly accessible to commuting facilities, and, most importantly, its growth has lacked any true trading center.

Population

The 1950 township census showed population of 3,400 people. Adjusting for housing starts through 1958 and, assuming an average family of 3.7 persons, a population of 5,400 was estimated for the latter year or approximately 1,460 families at the time the township was surveyed. A five-year projection of a continued level rate of growth would yield 6,800 people, or about 1,840 families.

Income

From *Sales Management* and local sources, family income was estimated at some $6,300 annually. Referring to the Federal Reserve Board Survey of Consumer Finances, it was estimated that the total potentials for 1,460 families at this income level would be $450,000 in demand accounts and $1,150,000 in savings. If totally attainable, this potential of $1.6 million could support a very modest branch and give some promise for the future. These figures could be adjusted upward somewhat to allow for underreporting but they could also be viewed hesitantly in respect to the rather young age of most of the new population. On balance they probably yield fair indication of total potential.

Trade Area and Established Habits

Attainable business seldom approaches total potential. This is further emphasized by the convenience shopping aspect of retail banking. Against an estimated $5.3 million of retail sales spending by the township's population, only some $500,000 was being spent locally. The situation was visually evident through the existence of only forty-one small enterprises operating in the whole township. Most important, there was no real trading center and the enterprises were scattered along two more or less major roads. Commercial business beyond the small store level was nonexistent.

Applying the convenience shopping principle and judging the nature of the population by observation, it was evident that the people were willing and able to travel to adjacent communities for their shopping and banking needs.

Although a large (5.5 square miles) and attractive township, it was evident that a branch there would attract only a small percentage of total potential. A concentration of shopping activity together with predictable growth might make a future venture worthwhile. However, this would best be preceded by an analysis of existing business in the township and by a measured observation of traffic patterns.

Conclusions

This is a fairly typical case of a bank seeking avenues of growth rather than one of economic need leading to banking office consideration. It is further of interest in that although family income is lower than in, say, accepted new Bank G (described in the next chapter), the population of Township F is probably of a more professional makeup. It only shows that more successful individuals are less likely to have more than one working member of the family and, second, that this newer, younger group is probably more of a current nonsaver type than was the case with Bank A.

Most important is the fact that potential can be measured only in relation to an established trading point or, more recently, to a strategic access point. Neither of these exists, in this case at the present stage of development.

VII

Successful new banks

In this chapter two situations will be described to show the actual accomplishments of new banks for which charters have been granted in recent years. Naturally, each has distinct characteristics. An attempt will be made to compare these cases with the generalized methods of estimating deposit potential. Other appropriate comments will be made. In each case the organizers prepared their own applications with some help from correspondent banks. There was at least one lawyer in each group.

BANK G[1]

Bank G was granted a charter based on favorable reaction to its incorporators and the following salient statistics: Town G is located in a thickly populated county which is a component of a large metropolitan area. County G and Town G had shown rapid growth since World War II. Town G had grown 54 per cent from 1940 to 1950, showing one of the highest rates of growth for a municipality within the state. Population in 1950 was 38,000 and at the time of chartering was estimated at

50,000. Other indications of growth included value of new building, which was running approximately $7 million per annum, ratables had more than doubled since 1940,[2] and postal receipts had quadrupled to $500,000.[3] The local telephone company indicated that 90 per cent of residences had phones, with collections 99.4 per cent current.

Family income was estimated at $8,400 average for an estimated 12,000 families and 3,000 individuals, or 15,000 spending units. Disposable income for the municipality was estimated at $72 million with sales within the municipality at only $50 million, indicating some drawoff to adjacent larger trading centers.

The estimated labor force was 22,500 of which 11,500 were industrial workers and the remainder white-collar sales personnel.[4]

Commercial trade consisted of 358 establishments with sales of approximately $50 million. On a per capita basis, sales were only $1,000 as compared to $1,400 for the state as a whole,[5] again indicating some drawoff.

Industrially, the municipality enjoyed sixteen AAA1 companies and a host of smaller companies with an estimated gross value of manufacture of $95 million.[6]

Local analysis of tax maps and other information indicated that the municipality was about two-thirds developed, indicating further expansion. There was practically no slum area in the town and the income characteristics of its residents were rather uniform.

The municipality had developed an obvious trading center, created by the right-angle intersection of two main roads. While the municipality had a total area of ten square miles, not all of this could be considered a logical trading area because of the proximity of other established trading centers. At the time of chartering there was a well-established commercial bank, located on the principal corner in town, with deposits of $21.5 million. In addition there was a branch of a large savings and loan association one block from the center on a main thoroughfare. Other substantial commercial banks were established in nearby trading areas in all directions.

The Balance Sheet and Income Figures on pages 92–95 indicate the relative success of this new bank, which started with capital and reserves of $352,000.

This bank has obviously been quite successful. It is also interesting to note that the competitor bank in town, which had deposits of $21.5 million at time of opening, had deposits of $27.3 million when the new bank was two years old.

The location of this bank is worthy of note: while the trading center was fixed at the intersection of the two main streets, there was little parking within two blocks of that point. Bank G chose a location three blocks from the key intersection, which allowed both adequate parking and drive-in facilities. This location was not, however, within normal walking distance of most of the stores.

Management of Bank G was aggressive and sales-minded from the start. The maximum allowable rate was paid on savings from the beginning and a vigorous advertising campaign was conducted.

As to operations, it can be seen that Bank G started making money on a current basis in its second six months and showed a small profit for the third six months. Recoupment of surplus and initial expenditures, however, did not arrive until the third year. Dividends were paid in the fourth year.

Loan figures cannot be used as a guide since loans were obtained from outside sources to boost earning power. This is a fairly frequent procedure with new banks and prevents any real generalization concerning local loan demand.

BANK G — BALANCE SHEETS

Day Before Opening

ASSETS		LIABILITIES	
Due from Banks	$ 65,000	Common Stock	$220,000
Gov't Securities	199,000	Surplus	110,000
Furn. & Fixtures	43,000	Organization Exp.	22,000
Leasehold Imp.	32,000	Total	$352,000
Prepaid	1,200	Income	1,700
Total	$340,200		
Gen'l Expense	13,500		
	$353,700		$353,700

Close of Business 1st Day

ASSETS		LIABILITIES	
Due from Banks	$252,000	Common Stock	$220,000
Gov't Securities	199,000	Surplus	110,000
Cash	82,000	Org. Expense	22,000
Furn. & Fixtures	43,000	Total	$352,000
Leasehold Imp.	32,000	Demand Dep.	192,000
Prepaid	1,200	Savings Dep.	77,000
Total	$609,200	Total	$621,000
Gen'l Expense	13,500	Income	1,700
	$622,700		$622,700

Six Months

ASSETS		LIABILITIES	
Due from Banks	$ 324,000	Common Stock	$ 220,000
Gov't Securities	1,354,000	Surplus	83,000 (1)
Loans	753,000	Reserves	7,000 (1)
Cash	56,000		310,000
Furn. & Fixtures	78,000	Demand Dep.	963,000
Leasehold Imp.	33,000	Treas. T & L	52,000
Accrued Interest	10,000	Treas. Checks	55,000
Prepaid	5,000	Payables	3,000
Total	$2,613,000	Savings Dep.	1,104,000
		Time, Open A/C	65,000
		Clubs	47,000
		Unearned Int.	14,000
		Total	$2,613,000

Twelve Months

ASSETS		LIABILITIES	
Due from Banks	$ 312,000	Common	$ 220,000
Gov't Securities	1,440,000	Surplus	69,000 (2)
Loans	2,122,000	Reserves	10,000 (2)
Cash	120,000		$ 299,000
Other Bonds	50,000	Demand Dep.	1,614,000
Furn. & Fixtures	78,000	Treas. T & L	93,000
Leasehold Imp.	35,000	Treas. Checks	77,000
Accrued Int.	10,000	Payables	9,000
Prepaid	6,000	Savings Dep.	1,840,000
Total	$4,173,000	Cert. of Dep.	100,000
		Time, Open A/C	65,000
		Clubs	21,000
		Unearned Int.	55,000
		Total	$4,173,000

BANK G—BALANCE SHEETS

Eighteen Months

ASSETS		LIABILITIES	
Due from Banks	$ 345,000	Common Stock	$ 220,000
Gov't Securities	1,878,000	Surplus	69,000(3)
Loans	2,887,000	Reserves	14,000(4)
Cash	134,000		$ 303,000
Other Securities	152,000	Demand Dep.	1,950,000
Furn. & Fixtures	87,000	Treas. T & L	104,000
Leasehold Imp.	34,000	Payables	127,000
Accrued Int.	11,000	Savings Dep.	2,381,000
Prepaid	6,000	Cert. of Dep.	16,000
Total	$5,534,000	Time, Open A/C	100,000
		Clubs	393,000
		Unearned Int.	76,000
		Treas. Checks	70,000
		Total	$5,520,000

Two Years

ASSETS		LIABILITIES	
Due from Banks	$ 492,000	Common Stock	$ 220,000
Gov't Securities	2,306,000	Surplus	88,000(5)
Loans	3,283,000	Reserves	17,000(6)
Cash	203,000		$ 325,000
Other Securities	128,000	Demand Dep.	2,504,000
Furn. & Fixtures	91,000	Treas. T & L	112,000
Leasehold Imp.	34,000	Treas. Checks	68,000
Accrued Int.	14,000	Payables	7,000
Prepaid	4,000	Savings Dep.	2,890,000
Total	$6,555,000	Cert. Dep.	100,000
		Time, Open A/C	407,000
		Clubs	46,000
		Unearned Int.	70,000
		Suspense	26,000
		Total	$6,555,000

(3) Not adjusted—accruals changed to yearly basis.
(4) Adjusted to allowable debt reserve.
(5) Adjusted reflecting year's operations.
(6) Same as (4).

BANK G—INCOME STATEMENTS

At Opening		Six Months		Second Six Months		First Year	
Expenses	$13,500	Gen'l Expenses	$53,000	Gen'l Expense	$66,000	Org. Exp. Net	$11,800
Bond Income	1,700	Interest Paid	7,000	Bad Debt & Reserve	5,000	1st Six Months	20,600
Net Loss	$11,800		$60,000	Int. Paid	14,000	2nd Six Months	19,000
					$85,000	Total	$51,400
INITIAL CAPITAL		Loan Int.	9,900	Loan Interest	40,000		
Common Stock	$220,000	Bond Int.	12,600	Bond Int.	17,000	SURPLUS RECONCILIATION	
Surplus	110,000	Commissions	5,100	Comm. & Svce. Chg.	9,000	Beginning Surp.	
Reserves Org. Exp.	22,000	Security Profits	11,800		$66,000	& Reserves	$132,000
Total	$352,000		$39,400	Net Loss	$19,000	Losses—1st Year	51,400
		Net Loss	$20,600				$ 80,600
						Reported Surp.	
						& Reserves	79,000
						Reserve Adjust.	$ 1,600

BANK G—INCOME STATEMENTS

Third Six Months

Loan Interest	$ 74,000
Bond Interest	19,000
Commission & Charges	15,000
Total Income	$108,000
General Expenses	79,000
Interest Paid	21,000
	$100,000
Net Income	$ 8,000

Second Year (Full)

Loan Interest	$168,000
Bond Interest	44,000
Commission & Charges	33,000
Total Income	$245,000
General Expenses	173,000
Interest Paid	49,000
	$222,000
Net Income	$ 23,000

Surplus Reconciliation (Full Year)

Year End Surplus & Reserves	$105,000
Previous Year End	79,000
Added to Surplus	$ 26,000
Adjustments	$ 3,000

Hypothetical Comparison

A hypothetical comparison for the deposit level attained by Bank G as of two full years after opening has been conservatively compiled as follows:

Individual and Family Market		3,000 units
Commercial		75 commercial units
Industrial		Nothing
Public	Federal Government	2% of total deposits
	State	Nothing
	Municipal	30% of total working funds

Individual and Family ($8,400 average family income)				
Demand Deposits	3,000 @ $ 590	=	$1,770,000
Savings	3,000 @ 880	=	2,640,000
Commercial (Average $1,200)	75 @ 1,200	=	90,000
Municipal (Actual experience of Town average $800,000)			240,000
Totals to this Point		Demand	$2,100,000
		Savings	2,640,000
			4,740,000
		Federal Government	94,000
		Total	4,834,000
		Actual	5,134,000

There is, of course, considerable rounding and arbitrary selection in the preparation of such a comparison. It is based on a firsthand study of the trade area, which gives a feel for the market not possible in an abstract sense. The principal deviation in Bank G's case apparently was a better than usual penetration in the commercial field based on aggressive solicitation and on a conservative history concerning the existing commercial bank in town.

Further, the comparison has its greatest use in highlighting the preponderant importance of individual accounts.

BANK H

This is a useful case to consider as it represents a rather marginal situation in terms of strength to support a new bank.

Decision to grant a charter was undoubtedly influenced by unusual circumstances, which for the purpose of this study is perhaps fortunate. Bank H is in reality a component of a larger existing bank with several offices. The larger Bank H is unusual in that each of its offices operates as a separate entity with its own portfolio, reserve accounts, and capital structure. Earnings also are computed separately and the bank is combined only for dividend consideration and reporting purposes. In this case initial capital was supplied by the existing bank, and expenses to date of opening were carried by the larger bank. Specific comment covering this will follow presentation of the balance sheet data.

Economic Circumstances

The town in question is a small one, population 2,000, and the larger trade area within this bank's potential market is estimated at 6,000. In addition, this town is a rapidly growing summer resort with a peak estimated seasonal population of 20,000. Industry is primarily agriculture and fishing, plus the hotel and entertainment business connected with the tourist season.

Family income for year-round residents averaged $4,200, while the income of summer residents undoubtedly averaged a good deal higher, being drawn from the middle and upper income groups of metropolitan areas which are within weekend vacationing distance.

Dun & Bradstreet rated 193 enterprises in Town H. Only two names were rated AA1 and these were branches of multiplant concerns. Total value of physical production from fishing was estimated at $3 million; agricultural production within the trade area, primarily chickens and garden crops, was estimated at $12 million; revenue from resort business was estimated at $4.5 million—total trade area revenues of $19.5 million.

An existing bank in the same town had an attained deposit level of $2,215,000 at the time of chartering. Six other banks within a radius of twenty miles had aggregate deposits of $21.6 million. The trading area for these other banks was of a similar agricultural nature without any measurable extent of the resort feature.

The competitor bank in this town was located on a dead-end street in the center of the commercial-resort area. Only street parking and foot traffic provide access to this bank. Bank H chose a location about one mile out of town on the main artery, in a position to intercept agricultural and tourist automobile business as it came from the highway. And adequate parking and drive-in facilities were provided. Walk-in business could not be expected to be much of a factor at Bank H's location. On page 99 are balance sheets of Bank H as of opening date and at six-month intervals through eighteen months of operation.

Before generalizing, several comments are pertinent regarding the preceding balance sheets.

These are not finalized balance sheets, since they were taken at somewhat arbitrary intervals to show developments at six-month stages. As a result, the three sets of operating expense and income figures are approximately semiannual figures. Income figures for the sixth month and the eighteenth month do not include bond interest, whereas the twelve-month figures do. By estimate, uniform figures would raise income by approximately $600 per half year for the sixth- and eighteenth-month reports and a $300 reduction at twelve months. Apparently interest was accrued semiannually.

The initial figures represent quite a misrepresentation in terms of an independent bank. Initial capital of $200,000 was provided, and in addition there was provided $50,000 of undivided profits, which is reflected as a net figure in the sixth month and in subsequent statements. Also, subsequent statements reflect the expenditure on real estate and furniture and fixtures of $138,000. Considering these figures, the opening-

BANK H – BALANCE SHEETS

1st Day—Close of Business

Cash	$ 60,300	Capital Stock	$ 30,000
Due from Banks	180,500	Surplus	170,000
Gov't Securities	—	Demand Dep.	34,600
Loans	200	Time Dep.	6,400
Total	$241,000	Total	$241,000

Six Months (Height of season)

Cash	$ 55,000	Capital Stock	$ 30,000
Due from Banks	267,000	Surplus	170,000
Gov't Securities	99,000	Undivided Pft.	28,600
Loans	650,000	Demand Dep.	765,000
Real Estate	148,000	Time Dep.	262,100
Furn. & Fixtures	34,000	Reserves	6,900
Operating Exp.	18,000	Int. Income	7,900*
		Other Income	500
Total	$1,271,000	Total	$1,271,000

Twelve Months

Cash	$ 80,000	Capital Stock	$ 80,000
Due from Banks	144,000	Surplus	144,000
Gov't Securities	99,500	Undivided	99,500
Loans	771,000	Demand Dep.	771,000
Real Estate	145,800	Time Dep.	145,800
Furn. & Fixtures	31,500	Reserves	31,500
Operating Exp.	20,000	Int. Income	14,100*
		Other Income	800
Total	$1,291,800	Total	$1,291,800

Eighteen Months (Height of season)

Cash	$ 94,900	Capital Stock	$ 30,000
Due from Banks	342,400	Surplus	170,000
Gov't Securities	99,700	Undivided	10,900
Other Securities	25,000	Demand Dep.	1,024,000
Loans	1,086,000	Time Dep.	583,000
Real Estate	144,400	Reserves	6,900
Furn. & Fixtures	29,500	Int. Income	14,200*
Operating Expenses	17,800	Other Income	700
Total	$1,839,700	Total	$1,839,700

* Not Comparable.

day balance sheet would appear as follows if this operation had been an independent one:

Cash	$ 60,300	Capital Stock	$ 30,000
Due from Banks	180,500	Surplus	170,000
Loans	200	Additional	
Real Estate	149,000	Contributed Surplus	198,000
Furn. & Fixtures	34,000	Demand Deposit	34,600
Organization Expenses	15,000*	Time Deposit	6,400
Total	$439,000	Total	$439,000

* Estimated.

This difference of $198,000 apparently was absorbed by the over-all bank as expense, allowing this office to start from the day of opening with its basic capital of $200,000 plus $50,000 of undivided profits. Most of this money, $184,000, went into real estate which was in effect provided free of charge insofar as the records of this semiautonomous unit were concerned. The same was true of organization expenses which did not appear on the opening books of Bank H. Since the building constructed was rather elaborate, a truer picture of the individual bank's position can be obtained if it is considered that the bank actually started with a capital of $448,000.

The seasonal aspects of Bank H's business distort somewhat the picture as reflected in the balance sheets. The sixth-month and eighteenth-month reports represent a high point in the tourist season. This is reflected primarily in demand deposits and loans.

Bank H's expenses have been internally estimated at $6,500 per month. Against this, at present rates, a deposit level of $2 million and a loan volume of $1.3 million are required to break even. While these levels are expected during the next peak season (twenty-fourth month), they cannot reasonably be expected on the average for at least two years, or into the fourth year of operation.

Leaving out the $198,000 of estimated initial expenditures, this bank has experienced a net operating loss (no income tax considerations) of approximately $42,000 when the figures for eighteen months are accrued. To be sustained as an independent bank, Bank H would have required a total capital of approximately $500,000 (undivided profits of $100,000) and a very patient group of stockholders.

It is interesting to compare a deposit potential estimate for the trading area of 6,000 with the attainment of eighteen months.

Hypothetical Comparison

This comparison will follow the same format as in Bank G. The averages for individual accounts apply more fairly to two full years, by which time the bank will have a fair measure of maturity. However, the eighteen-month figures that are available represent the height of seasonal activity, and thus the comparison will not be too badly distorted.

Individual and Family Market		1,200 units		
Commercial		50 units		
Industrial		Nothing		
Public	Federal Government	2% of deposits		
	State	Nothing		
	Municipal	40% of total working funds		
Individual and Family ($4,200 average family income)				
Demand Deposits		1,200 @ $270	=	$ 324,000
Savings		1,200 @ 480	=	576,000
Commercial (Average $800)		50 @ 800	=	40,000
Municipal (Actual experience of Town $250,000)				100,000
Totals to this Point			Demand	464,000
			Savings	576,000
				$1,040,000
			Federal Government	20,000
			Total	$1,060,000
			Actual	$1,580,000

As can be seen, the relative proportions of demand and savings deposits do not follow the national averages in this instance. Interest paid in this area remains at 2 per cent and there are practically no savings institutions as such in the area. And the picture is somewhat further blurred by the transfer to this bank of accounts in its trade area from the adjacent branch of the larger bank about eight miles distant. Under these circumstances the hypothetical comparison probably overestimated the number of year-round family units in this bank's market. The higher level of demand deposits, it was learned, are attributable to more well-to-do seasonal residents and merchants plus help from the larger bank's other components.

VIII
New banks—refused charters

This chapter will describe two communities in which charter applications were refused. To the best of the writer's knowledge, neither charter was refused for reasons of doubt about the character or integrity of the organizers. Therefore, the reason for charter refusal was economic. A description of the community will be provided for each case, together with pertinent excerpts from the ruling denying the application.

Interestingly, in each of these cases professional research firms were employed to appraise the potential of the proposed bank's trade area. In each case these reports were affirmative as to the area's need for and ability to support a bank.

CASE I

Township I is on the periphery of a large metropolitan trading area. It is a large land area (4.5 square miles) between two major spokes of the wheel that makes up the metropolitan area. Major railroad and highway lines had caused intensive development of communities along the spokes to distances well beyond Township I. This township was not too far from the center of the metropolitan area but prewar development had bypassed it. Coming out of World War II, Township I was largely farms.

Population has soared since the war, increasing from 2,000 in 1940 to 4,300 in 1950, with a 1955 estimate of 9,000. This development has been primarily through the conversion of farms into lower and middle range single-family housing developments. As of 1955, the township was 55 per cent developed and had a total of 2,600 residential structures. A master plan had established zoning areas and requirements for the orderly development of the remaining land area.

There were 21 industrial firms at the time of the survey, occupying 6 per cent of the total land area. Railroad sidings and highway facilities make this an attractive location and the master plan made allowance for a better than 100 per cent increase in over-all industrial land use. Among the 21 industries were three large plants of nationally known firms, the remainder being small manufacturers with a capital of $100,-000 or less.

Retail and commercial establishments numbered 49, most of which could be classified as small local stores. These establishments are scattered throughout the township but primarily in three separate small trade centers.

Wealth Characteristics

Township I has a younger population and a larger-sized family than is true for the county and state as a whole. Approximately 44 per cent of the population is between 21 and 44 years of age, with 34 per cent under 21 and only 4 per cent over 65. The average family size is 3.55 persons as compared to 3.48 for the county and 3.40 for the state.

Total income of families was estimated at $10.5 million. Median income is estimated at $3,930 as compared to $4,312 for the county as a whole. Distribution by income categories showed 9 per cent of families with incomes under $2,000; 59

per cent have incomes of $3,000–$5,900; 31 per cent have incomes over $5,000.

Retail sales by the 49 establishments are estimated at $2.5 million, or $1,030 per family as compared to a county average of $3,652.

Competition

There are fourteen banks within a three-mile radius of the center of Township I. These banks are located in the towns lying along the major spokes of the wheel on three sides of the township. There is no bank in the adjacent area on the fourth, or most distant, side. Total deposits of these banks are difficult to estimate because several are offices of multibranch banks located elsewhere. They are at least $100 million based on available statistics.

Definition of Trade Area

Township I is a long and irregular land area with its long axis running somewhat parallel to the established spokes on both sides of it. Interviews and other research showed that families in the township tended to go at right angles to the long axis, doing their shopping and banking in the nearest established trade center in one of the two adjacent spokes of the wheel. One unusual feature that emphasized these sidewise flows of traffic was the existence of a limited access superhighway which cut the most densely populated third of the township away from the remaining two-thirds.

The organizers of Bank I recognized that there was no trading center for their township. They reasoned that a bank located at approximately the geographic center of the township would serve as a nucleus for such a center and that the evident buying power present plus indicated growth would bring appropriate commercial and retail establishments. They chose a location in a partly completed shopping center at this central point. Interestingly, although there were fourteen banks within three miles, none was less than two miles from this site.

Based on this site and a computation of equal travel time to other banking facilities, a larger trade area was defined. This area totaled 17 square miles with 7,000 families, of which 4.5 square miles and 2,500 families represented the township itself. On balance, the income characteristics of the larger area were similar to those of the township.

Deposit Estimates

Estimates for the township were made as follows:

SAVINGS

From the Federal Reserve *Survey of Consumer Finances* 31 per cent, or 537, of the 1,737 families earning less than $5,000 were considered negative savers. The remaining 1,200 families could be expected to save 12 per cent of total income, or $656,000.

Of the 798 families earning over $5,000, 41 per cent, or 327, were negative savers. The remaining 471 families would save 13 per cent of income, or $684,000. In the survey for this bank the research firm made the assumption that positive savers would keep 6 per cent of total income in savings accounts, in this instance $670,000.

CHECKING ACCOUNTS

The assumption was made that balances in checking accounts from families with incomes of less than $5,000 would be negligible. For those families earning more than $5,000, it was estimated that 75 per cent, or 598, of the 798 families would carry average balances of $645,000.

RETAIL DEPOSITS

The research firm estimated that the 49 businesses in the township would maintain deposits of $1,500–$2,000, for a total of $85,000.

INDUSTRIAL DEPOSITS

No deposits were expected from the three larger industries, the 18 smaller firms were estimated at $2,500–$3,000 each, for a total of $50,000.

The Larger Trade Area

The larger trade area as defined contained 2,360 families with incomes over $5,000 and 5,260 families with lower incomes. Following the reasoning previously applied, the research firm estimated potentials of $1.9 million in savings. No estimates were made for outside retail or industrial deposits.

Application for charter was based on these figures showing total deposit potential from the defined trading area of $3.8 million. Initial capital was not defined at this point.

Supervisory Decision

Pertinent comments from the decision in this case are as follows:

"The Township has an area of 4.7 miles. Its population of 4,300 at the 1950 census increased to 7,550 by July 1 1956 as estimated by the state department of Economic Development.

"The address for which this application is made is the southwest corner of X Road and Y Drive. Actually the site is part of a tract of land located in the rear of some small stores fronting on Y Drive.

"I concur with the projection submitted by the experienced firm which made a study of A's present and potential prospects that its future is a promising one. . . .

"While the decision was under consideration, the attorney representing the incorporators requested a reopening of the hearing to enable them to present evidence of further industrial growth at A and, what is more important, evidence that a shopping center was about to be built there in which the proposed banking quarters would be located. The establishment of such a shopping center is, in the opinion of the department, the key to their whole case because of the effect it might be expected to have on the shopping and banking habits of the residents of A.

"A is surrounded by seven communities with easy access thereto by residents of A, all with banks and most, if not all, with shopping areas. Over the years, because of the lack of stores in A, most residents have done their buying in those municipalities and quite naturally have done their banking there. Consequently, a new bank in A to succeed would have to bring about a change in both the established shopping and banking habits of its residents. In my opinion, it could not do so without shopping facilities."

Unfortunately, although this is a good sample case, the hearing and decision did not come to grips with the basic question of demonstrated potential. They do, however, clarify the point that a center of commercial concentration must precede the establishment of a new unit bank. (As a matter of interest, the application was filed twenty-three months before a final decision was obtained.)

Hypothetical Comparison

In this case comparison will be made to the potential as estimated by the outside consulting firm which surveyed the market for the charter application. This study assumes the present scattered commercial situation within the town.

This comparison is especially useful from several points of view. The professional survey put forth totals based on the complete potential of the possible trade area without discussing the degree to which this business would be retained by existing banks. In a less important vein, the survey assumed

Individual and Family Market		1,200 units		
Commercial		25 units		
Industrial		Nothing		
Public	Federal Government	2% of total deposits		
	State	Nothing		
	Municipal	100% of total working funds		
Individual and Family ($4,000 average family income)				
Demand Deposits		1,200 @ $ 270	=	$ 324,000
Savings		1,200 @ 480	=	576,000
Commercial (Average $1,000)		25 @ 1,000	=	25,000
Municipal (Actual experience of Town average $200,000)				200,000
Totals to this Point			Demand	549,000
			Savings	576,000
				$1,125,000
			Federal Government	20,000
			Total	$1,145,000
			Survey Estimate	$3,800,000

that all the retail enterprises would bank with "I" as would several of the smaller manufacturers against whom the objection of prior bank loyalties and convenience could be levied. Statistically, the survey followed a more correct procedure than is done here in estimating individual potentials. These should properly be computed as potential within income brackets rather than on a lumped average basis as has been used here for simplification. While simpler, averages tend to understate results as compared to computations by brackets.

It is felt that the estimated potential of $1,045,000 is much more realistic for the time and under the circumstances. Since this level would provide meager support for a complete bank, it would appear that the decision was a sound one.

CASE J

Township J also is on the periphery of a large metropolitan area. It is not on any direct line of transportation to the metropolitan center and cannot be considered a commuting town in that sense. Rather, Township J is more of a residential center within driver or bus commuting range of an industrial center which is located in one quadrant of the larger metropolitan circle.

Before the war Township J had included a mixture of year-round and summer residents, the latter because of its attractive hilly country interspersed with small lakes. Population in 1940 was 3,200. By 1950 population had grown to 4,600, and a survey estimate in 1957 placed population at 8,200. With this growth, much of the population became year-round residents.

There were 124 commercial establishments in the township with total sales estimated at $22 million. These figures were based on the 1954 census of commercial trade by the Bureau of the Census plus projections for a new shopping center since established and plus normal growth. Township J enjoyed a good concentration of commercial activity in its downtown section. Pressure on this downtown section has been alleviated, however, by the new shopping center which is nearby and offers excellent parking facilities.

Wealth Characteristics

Latest data available estimated 1956 average family income for Township J at $7,400 per year.[1] This compares with a figure of $4,200 for the county as a whole as reported in the 1950 census.[2] While the 1956 figure seems high in relation to the county average, Township J is relatively free of low-income areas, whereas several older sections of the county contain substantial blocks of lower income population. Unfortunately, there were no reliable percentage breakdowns of families by income bracket.

Assessed Valuations

Total assessed valuations in Township J were $10.5 million as of 1955. Total tax collections, including delinquents, have averaged 99 per cent, with current collections averaging 95 per cent. Moody's rating for township school bonds was A.

Competition

Within a four-mile radius of the center of Township J there were seven bank offices. All were branches of larger banks headquartered in other areas. One of these offices was located in the presently established trading center of Township J. This banking office had been an independent bank achieving a deposit level of $7.7 million prior to its merger four years earlier. All of these banking offices could be classed as regional-residential and none had any exceptional industrial business.

Trade Area

The approach taken in this instance in defining the trade area was an interesting one. Per capita retail sales for the state as a whole were $1,100 based on the 1954 commercial census. Using this figure, the research firm concluded that the population of the trade area was at least 20,000. The survey further stated that the local figures did not include certain larger purchases such as clothing and furniture, these purchases being made in nearby metropolitan areas. Using an assumed 60 per cent of total purchases on a local basis, it was concluded that the population behind the estimated local sales of $22 million was 33,000.

Utilizing local traffic flow maps, the survey proceeded to define certain percentages of adjacent communities as part of the trade area. Demonstrating that per capita sales in these adjacent communities were substantially lower and utilizing the traffic flow survey, an intensive trade area of 17,000 people was defined. The differential was termed the "extensive trade area" and for the purposes of the survey the figure of 17,000 was used to estimate the bank's potential market.

Deposit Potentials

This survey, assuming that the average income per family in the trade area was $7,500, proceeded to make deposit estimates for a trade area of 17,000 people. On the basis of 3.5 persons per family, the resultant 4,800-family market was set against the Federal Reserve Board's *Survey of Consumer Finances*. The resulting totals were: demand deposits, $3,325,-000; savings deposits, $5,545,000.

This survey made two further comments on deposit potentials from individuals. Noting that the Federal Reserve Board's survey lumped all incomes above $5,000 in the surveys covering bank accounts, this survey assumed that the amount of holdings rose faster than family income in the higher brackets and that therefore the figures available were actually low for the case in point. Also it was pointed out that the Federal Reserve survey had cautioned that people tended to understate liquid holdings and that the table figures were probably low. With these facts in hand, the survey concluded that the deposit potential from families was approximately $16 million.

Competitive Potential

The survey then concluded that $3 million of this total could be achieved by the proposed bank within five years. It also stated that the achievable commercial potential for the bank was $1 million. These figures, together with municipal deposits of $250,000, resulted in an estimated potential of $4,250,000 after five years. Interestingly, they estimated a total of only $2 million after three years of operation.

Supervisory Decision

Pertinent comments from the decision are as follows:

The Borough of B is the smallest municipality in upper X County having a land area of only 3.8 square miles. Its population of 4,600 at the 1950 census increased to 6,900 by July 1, 1957, according to the State Department of Conservation and Economic Development. While it has shared in the general economic and population growth during the past ten years, it has now reached a point where there is little room for further expansion. Its shopping area is largely concentrated on Y Avenue, a narrow street with limited, restricted parking.

As B developed, so did the municipalities in the surrounding area. The crowded situation of its shopping area and the lack of convenient parking, led to the development of five major shopping centers and neighboring municipalities located within three to four miles of the Borough of B.

B is no longer the hub of activity it was in the early forties.

Thus we find seven banking offices within a radius of four miles of the site of the proposed bank, these seven offices are in an area formerly served by three independent banks, and are all supervised and operated by experienced bankers who are well known and respected in this area.

I am of the opinion that B and surrounding areas have adequate and convenient banking service, that healthy competition exists between the already established banks, that the interests of the public will not be served to advantage by the establishment of an additional and new bank in B.

Hypothetical Comparison

Again, comparison will be against the results submitted by the independent survey.

Individual and Family Market		1,600 units
Commercial		40 units
Industrial		One directed
Public	Federal Government	2% of total deposits
	State	Nothing
	Municipal	25% of working funds

Industrial and Family ($7,400 average family income)

Demand Deposits	1,600 @ $ 590	=	$ 944,000
Savings	1,600 @ 880	=	1,408,000
Commercial (Average $1,200)	40 @ 1,200	=	48,000
Industrial			30,000
Municipal (Actual experience of Town average $450,000)			100,000
Totals to this Point	Demand		1,122,000
	Savings		1,408,000
			$2,530,000
	Federal Government		50,000
	Total		$2,580,000
	Survey Estimate		$2,000,000 (3 yrs.)
			$3,000,000 (5 yrs.)

This survey would appear to be a realistic one, with the possible exception of an estimated commercial potential of $1,000,000 after five years. Based on comparable operations elsewhere Bank J probably could have become self-sustaining in time. The supervisory decision here stresses the competitive aspect both for the proposed bank and for its competitors. This is heightened by the fact that the competition stems from large multibranch units and that rate competition is presently a factor in the area. In sum, Bank J is a borderline situation in which there were apparently no clear-cut answers as to whether the area needed or could fully support a new bank.

IX

Do it yourself

All the foregoing text has been illustrative of specific experience in specific cases. While an attempt was made to display the most important types of cases arising today, the fact remains that each situation is unique and must be considered within the context of its own peculiar circumstances. Therefore, the best contribution that can be made here is to suggest a sequence of procedures through which a reasonably objective appraisal can be made.

The objective of any systematic inquiry is to reduce the many variables in a problem to a few general principles. It is felt that some such truths have been obtained via the case reviews, but these should be stated before going on to the methods of investigation which an individual bank can utilize.

BASIC TRUTHS

1. The several sets of data, such as town ratables, value of manufactures, total payroll, etc., have no known measurable correlation to estimated deposit potential.

2. The sole set of aggregate statistics that can be applied

en masse is the deposit potential for individuals based on known income brackets, and these statistics must be refined for the characteristics of the local market. All other categories of deposits must be considered individually.

3. The realistic trading area must be based on an established specific central point. From this point selective interview is the only firm means for defining the periphery of a trade area.

4. Competitive inroads, especially in duplicating trade areas, cannot be determined in advance. The only truth that can be stated here is that people are extremely slow to change banking connections even though there is evident vocal dissatisfaction. One must especially beware of any reliance on individual promises and estimates in this regard.

DON'T DO IT YOURSELF

Having said this, it is now important to make one further division as to suggested effort. It is strongly recommended that organizers of new unit banks obtain outside help. The ability of such groups to appraise objectively their own situations is limited by their lack of actual banking experience and is clouded by their enthusiasm. Help can be forthcoming from correspondents and other interested bankers but these too are limited by prejudice, preconceived ideas which may not pertain in the area under question, and lack of analytical experience. This will be especially true in intensely competitive situations. The best solution is to obtain the services of a reputable outside consultant. In a competitive situation charter applications are liable to be contested, which means that hearings will be held. There is both a need and a duty to provide the best possible information, since the investments of local citizens will be involved. Aside from the possibility of wasting money on poorly conceived applications, larger criteria must be considered. They are: does the area need a bank? can the area support a bank and will there be capable management?

The supervisory authorities are strong in their desire that only deserving cases be brought to the hearing stage. This is not the type of business which should be reduced to lawyer argument and political pressure. Objectivity, to the greatest possible extent, is necessary both to sound growth of the banking system and to the hopes of aspiring charter groups. As a practical matter, interested bankers who might be qualified will be extremely reluctant to become involved in public hearings because of the many interests which they have to consider. For these reasons it is strongly recommended that outside consultants be hired.

Further, it is suggested that such consultants be employed for a preliminary feasibility study before any other money is spent. If the preliminary study is encouraging, subsequent procedure will be evident; if not, substantial money and human energy will have been saved. There are exceptions, of course, and it is hoped that the following will be helpful to those groups which wish to do their own work.

Know Thyself

Having warned new unit banks against going it alone, so to speak, it is now proper to discuss existing banks that would seek to investigate new branch locations. The basic reason why existing banks can be encouraged to prepare their own surveys is that they have at hand the information on which to base them. Indeed this is more a suggested internal examination than a branch search per se. The potential of a proposed branch can be properly appraised only after a bank knows the characteristics and location of its existing business. Such knowledge will provide a far better indication of local banking characteristics than any outside survey can hope to provide. If a new branch is then indicated, it will be based on an extrapolation of known local characteristics. This is where the do-it-yourself doctrine can be applied and will pay for itself in improved understanding even if no new branches are indicated. It is high time for a major industry such as banking to know its basic commodity in other than aggregate form.

Self-analysis will confirm or change preconceived notions about account location and size. It should point up areas for greater effort and perhaps also indicate some areas of fruitless activity. Further, there is the defensive aspect. In an era of increasing competition it is vital to know the distribution and nature of one's customers so as to properly appraise the importance of competitive moves.

THE QUESTIONS

The questions are: What is the true trading area, what is its total banking potential, and against these what is the actual attainment of the bank in each deposit category? The answers will be their own indication of the course of action to be taken. The do-it-yourself procedure will be followed in relation to the circumstances of an actual but unidentified bank. An effort will be made to avoid unnecessary or repetitive detail consistent with clarity of description.

Bank K has two offices, well located in the centers of two almost contiguous residential communities. Each office enjoys adequate parking and each community can be characterized as a limited-convenience shopping center for commuters to two fairly distant metropolitan areas. Bank K has some $6 million in savings deposits, paying the maximum allowable rate, and some $7.2 million of demand moneys. There is no competition in the two towns except a $2-million savings and loan association located in the larger of the two towns with a current dividend rate of 3¼ per cent.

The Use of the Maps

The biggest virtue of using maps is that it forces consistent consideration of the problem. Initially it is useful simply to plot the area showing bank locations, thickly settled areas, and major routes of travel. Map on page 119 shows the two communities served by Bank K.

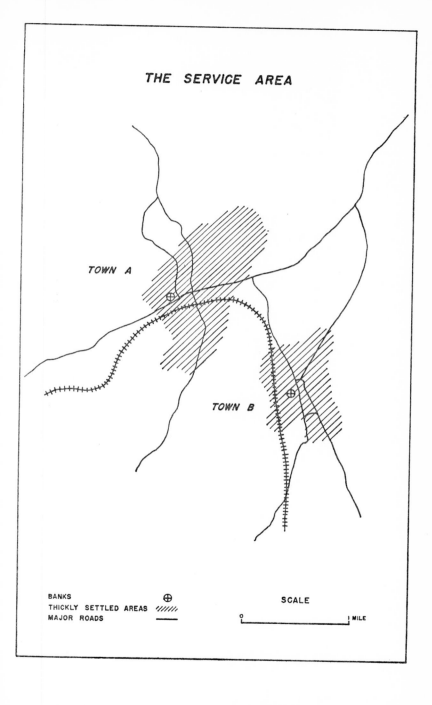

THE SERVICE AREA

TOWN A

TOWN B

BANKS ⊕
THICKLY SETTLED AREAS /////
MAJOR ROADS ——————

SCALE

0   1 MILE

A second step is to replot the map on a smaller scale to show the nearest competing institutions and to define the trading area on the basis of equal driving time. This is shown on the map on page 121.

The third step is suggested by the second; it is a check on the positive valence habits by selective interview along the suggested fringe of the reduced map. The outlying areas except to the southeast were all sparsely settled and fairly easy to determine. The settled area in the southeast revealed a very mixed pattern with a stronger valence to the city some six miles farther south. Indeed Community B fared poorly on the positive valence basis even though it provided the closest banking facility by a margin of some three miles. Elsewhere the survey revealed a strong pull by the city to the northeast and a good pull by K in the area to the west.

SAMPLING AND SUBSTANCE

With this background it is now possible to compare the existence of actual bank business with the area of supposed positive valence. The procedure will be described in terms of the $6 million of savings accounts held by Bank K in approximately 3,000 accounts, or an average account of $2000.

Savings

A 20 per cent sampling of savings accounts was made, using the large-scale map. The sample was taken from the savings accounts maintained at the bank's office in Town A. A clerk went through the ledger cards and placed an x on the map for the location of each fifth account. Since the office in A had some 2,200 accounts, this represented a sample of about 440 which, statistically, is more than adequate. The results are shown on the map on page 122. The most striking result is the narrowness of the trade area; well over 75 per cent of the ac-

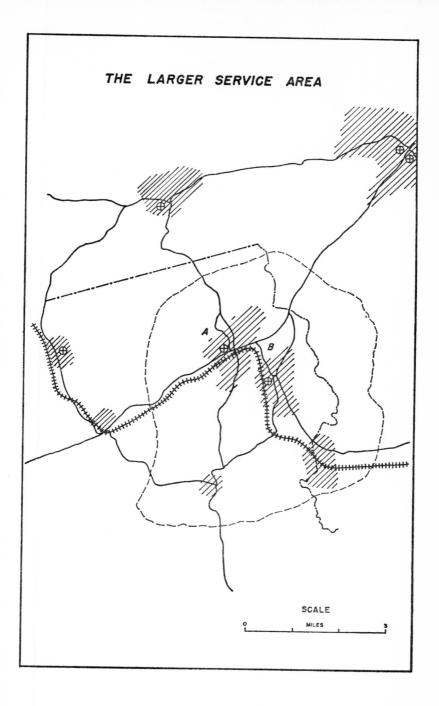

THE LARGER SERVICE AREA

A

B

SCALE

0   MILES   3

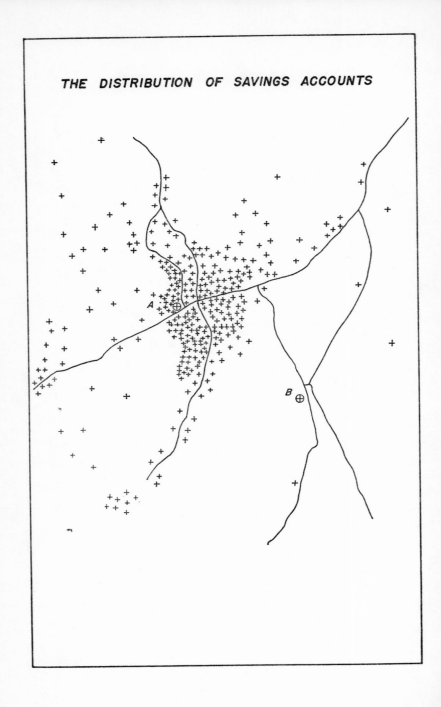

THE DISTRIBUTION OF SAVINGS ACCOUNTS

counts are located in Town A itself. This, it might be said, is a frequent discovery made in location sampling.

A second important calculation, especially in savings accounts, is the number of accounts per family, for there is no other way to measure the percentage of the total market that is held. It is recognized that family correlation will be incomplete but it is nonetheless a necessary minimum calculation. This can be done by a random investigation of one fifth of the ledger cards so long as the sample is alphabetically consecutive. From this hash-mark a tabulation of accounts can be made by moving horizontally for family multiples and vertically for the total number covered. In the case of Office A the result was some 2.2 accounts per family within the sample.

Special Checking

The second category to be geographically plotted was special checking accounts. These accounts tend to have a predictable average in the $100–$200 range nationally. This was true here with an average of some $180 per account. Since these are relatively homogeneous, averages may be fairly meaningful. Further, there is also some multiplicity of family accounts in this category and for the purposes of market analysis these figures are useful. A batch sample by both offices revealed 1.3 accounts per family. The geographic plotting of special checking accounts revealed a somewhat wider disbursion including fairly good penetration into the towns to the southeast and west—map on page 124. In total, Bank A had about 5,000 accounts for total balances of $900,000. While not too important as a source of balances, this category is indicative of convenience shopping habits as well as being a necessary weapon in any bank's arsenal. Incidentally, due to the homogeneity in this category and the large number of accounts, a smaller sample—say 10 per cent—is adequate for plotting purposes.

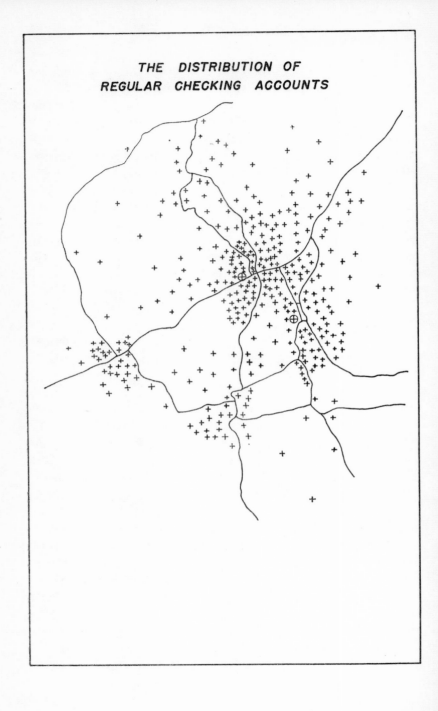

THE DISTRIBUTION OF
REGULAR CHECKING ACCOUNTS

Regular Demand

As previously indicated, the most unpredictable area and the area of greatest reward is regular demand accounts. Bank A had some $6.4 million in this over-all category exclusive of special checking. Of this, $350,000 was municipal, $50,000 was Federal and State government, and approximately $1.3 million was evidently commercial rather than individual. The commercial figures were obtained by total examination of the ledgers. This was not too difficult as the number of accounts was not too large—approximately 275 in all, for an average of $4,727. Averages here are not too meaningful as an examination of the ledgers will attest. While some generalizations are possible about certain enterprises such as pharmacies, barbershops, etc., it is best to consider even these individually in terms of new potential.

This leaves a relatively pure category of individual demand deposits of some $4.7 million. For future study, those ledgers selected as commercial were tagged with some identifying mark in order to exclude them from sampling within the individual category.

A 10 per cent sample of demand accounts was then plotted as map on page 126. The general distribution was somewhat wider than that for savings but somewhat narrower than that for special checking. It is not intended that these findings be considered generally true. They are not necessarily so and therefore self-analysis is a worthwhile field of investigation.

Further, in the collection of this sample the relative meaninglessness of averages was well illustrated. Although the average is higher than for special checking, it is too erratic for use except that it is the simplest single guide available. Indeed individual demand is the category most resistant to statistical analysis. As every banker realizes, there are a few extremely large accounts which more than offset a multitude which are or should be on a service charge basis. The median would be much more meaningful than the average but this

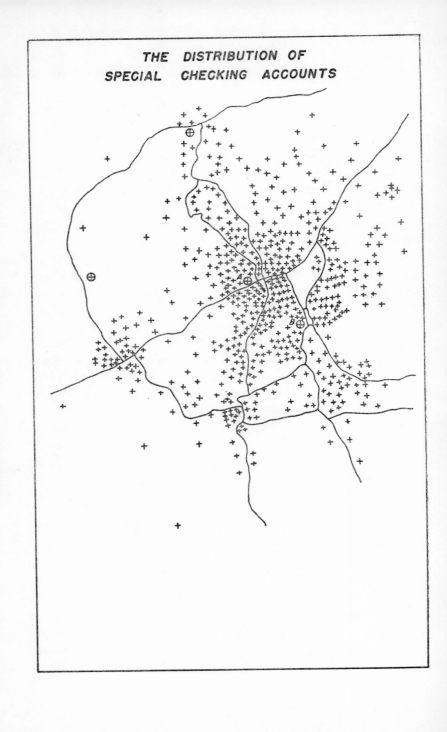

requires an entire listing in order of size and this is seldom available. In any event, Bank A had some 4,400 accounts aggregating $4.7 million, or an average of $1,068.

THE BUSINESS OF AVERAGES

It may well be said that most banks lack the facilities for properly computing such averages. This is true but it need not be so. Granted that many banks use minimum book balance as the basis for service charges. This is the easiest method for following accounts on a monthly basis but it is not useful for market analysis purposes. The minimum useful basis is averages for a reasonably typical month such as May or October. Book averages may be obtained by dividing total postings by the number of business days, with the figure written in pencil on the ledger. The problem of uncollected funds can most simply be handled by averaging the bank's deferred account and applying it pro rata to the bank's demand accounts. There is some misrepresentation here, to be sure, but it is the simplest method of approximating collected averages and a good portion of the errors will be offsetting. True knowledge of the actual position is one of the glaring weaknesses of banking but it is inherent in the subject matter. Although the suggested approximations are bound to contain error, these can be excused on the basis of consistent application and in light of the use to which the material is being put.

ACTUAL VS. POTENTIAL

By now the bank knows a little more about its important categories of deposits and their location. It also has a more firm understanding of actual attainment per account and per family in its trade area. It is now appropriate to consider these figures against the estimated potential of the trade area. Most importantly, by having analyzed its own circumstances the bank will have a far better knowledge of the per account and per family potential than can ever be obtained from any aggregate surveys such as those provided by the Federal Reserve Board.

Further Subdivision

As the examination proceeds it becomes evident that income brackets per family are the major consistent variable in account size. It is by no means the only variable, as Bank A discovered. Town A was the larger and more clearly divided of the two towns which were the heart of its trade area. Town A had a recently estimated population of 7,500 based on 1950 census data updated by local school figures. For purposes of potential analysis, Town A was replotted on a much larger scale map—map on page 129—and divided into four sections. The basis for the divisions was primarily family income, since it appeared to coincide with easily distinguishable geographic boundaries. In larger cities this could be by census tracts or even city blocks but in this instance, as it must be in smaller areas, it was based on local common sense. Four subdivisions considered were those areas of observable variation in family income as determined by housing value. Sections one and two were lower-income service-type families living in smaller houses in a more densely populated area. The third section consisted of postwar houses selling in the $20,000–$30,000 range. As a generalization, housing values are a good indication of current income if not of average age or of relative banking habits. The fourth section included a large land area, strongly zoned, and occupied by an upper-income group composed largely of commuters to the fairly distant metropolitan areas.

Measurement within Categories

With this subdivision based on observable circumstances, Bank A attempted to measure the actual attainment in each of the three deposit categories in order to compare actual at-

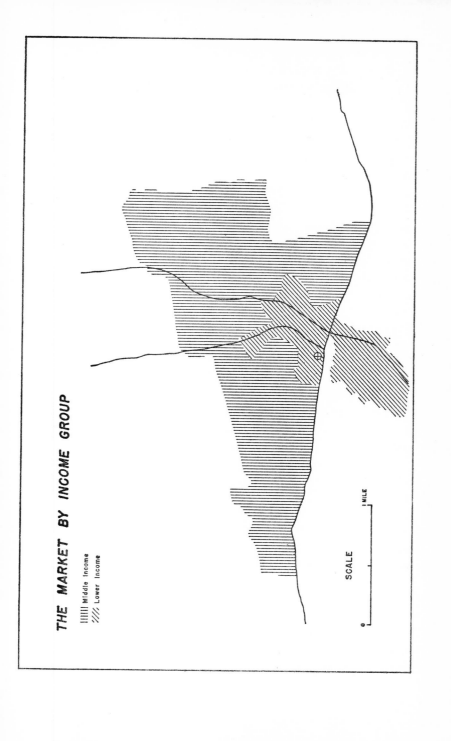

THE MARKET BY INCOME GROUP

||||| Middle Income
//// Lower Income

SCALE

0   1 MILE

tainment with area potential. The ledgers were re-examined at random to select a reasonably significant sample of business in each category within the four geographical areas. This can fairly easily be done by someone familiar with street addresses. This person must be instructed, however, so as to avoid any choosing by recognition of name—one way to achieve this is to use two people, one to announce the location and the second to categorize it, without reference to names. For purposes of simplification, sections A and B were characterized as lower income, section C as middle income, and section D as upper income.

In the savings account category the findings were summarized in Table 11.

Table 11

ACCOUNTS PER FAMILY & AVERAGE BALANCES

	No. of Accts.	Accts. per Family	Avg. Bal.	Totals
Lower Income	920	2.5	$2,015	$1,854,000
Middle Income	280	1.3	450	126,000
Upper Income	300	2.0	3,400	1,020,000
	1,500		$2,000	$3,000,000

The first thing to be recognized is that the accounts per family figure is incomplete at best since not all families carry all their business in one institution even if it has a clear location advantage. However, a division of the number of accounts per family into the number of accounts held in a given section does give a basic indication of the number of families in that area doing business with the bank. By simple division, then, a good approximation of the number of families in each area doing business with the bank can be obtained. This is far better than attempting to estimate the percentage of families which carry no account and trying to work backwards from an unverifiable assmuption. These calculations of families doing business were compared with the number of families residing in each area. The latter statistics were obtained from the local tax maps and the two were compared. Incidentally, the calculation of total families obtained by dividing the 7,500 population by an estimated 3.8 people per family, or 1,970 total families, checked out fairly well against the tax map count of 2,060 households. It was decided to use 2,000 as a working figure broken down and compared with actual attainment in Table 12.

Table 12

ACTUAL VS. EXTENDED POTENTIAL

	Total Families	Attained Family Bus.	Applied Family Average	Actual	Potential
Lower Income	750	368	$5,037	$1,854,000	$3,777,750
Middle Income	600	215	585	126,000	351,000
Upper Income	650	150	6,800	1,020,000	4,420,000
	2,000	733	$2,000	$3,000,000	$9,548,750

The potential figures are erroneous in one big way. Many families in each of the categories will carry no account at all, and thus the potential is overstated. For example, Federal Reserve studies show that in all categories, even the highest income brackets, a substantial percentage carry no account at all. As a cross check, the Federal Reserve tables, simplified to averages which include those having no accounts, were used as a rough cross check of Bank A's figures. Going back to the number of families in each area and applying the generalized income bracket figures as well as possible to the previously separated sections resulted in the Table 13 figures.

These figures are so far apart that several comments are warranted. First, the income figures are labeled by categories which are entirely too broad and unquestionably suffer from understatement. Further, they are difficut to apply. A return investigation of incomes in Bank A's lower-income group was prompted by these disparities. It revealed that on loan appli-

Table 13

ACTUAL VS. APPLIED POTENTIAL

	Income Bracket	Applied per Family Potential	Federal per Family Potential	Actual	Totals Applied	Federal
Lower Income	$3,000–5,000	$5,037	$480	$1,854,000	$3,777,750	$360,000
Middle Income	5,000–up	585	880	126,000	351,000	528,000
Upper Income	5,000–up	6,800	880	1,020,000	4,420,000	572,000

cations the lower-income group would indeed average about $4,400 in reported income but most of these families represented more than one job and underreporting was evident even in the loan applications. Second, the lumping of everything over $5,000 in family income has become almost meaningless since practically all families which are potential banking customers fall into this category. Third, there is the evident vast underreporting of account size by all families regardless of income. This is evident even in the actual attainment by Bank A which exceeds the Federal Reserve figures in every category.

The extent of this discrepancy was not expected. It exists, however, in what seems to be a fairly representative situation and so warrants even further investigation and comment to get closer to true levels. The characteristics of the lower-income people are most important. They are largely second- and third-generation immigrants mainly employed in higher forms of semi-skilled service-type jobs. These are people who would maintain most of their liquid assets in savings accounts if they are invested at all. The middle-income group as used here is in actuality a young professional-type population with relatively high incomes ($8,000–$12,000), with normally only the husband working and with fairly high family indebtedness. The upper-income group is a sophisticated one, familiar with many types of investment in which savings accounts play only a partial role.

Against these factors is the obvious fact that at best a substantial fraction (probably nowhere exceeding 75 per cent) has any savings accounts at all. Therefore, two things are known: (1) those families which do carry savings accounts run rather substantial family averages, except in the younger group which is busy paying off existing indebtedness; (2) a substantial portion of families in each observable economic category carries no savings accounts.

Bank A was unable to obtain a true survey on this, but after informal sampling came to the conclusion that 60 per cent of the total number of families was a realistic basis for potential as compared to business already held. On this basis, potential versus actual looked as in Table 14 for savings:

Table 14
ACTUAL VS. REALISTIC POTENTIAL

	Actual	60% of Potential
Lower Income	$1,854,000	$2,266,650
Middle Income	126,000	210,000
Upper Income	1,020,000	2,652,000
	$3,000,000	$5,128,650

In dollars and in numbers these studies showed that Bank A had achieved its best attainment in the lower-income group and its least in the upper-income group. Further, although the so-called middle held the least interest at present, growth here was evident and numerical attainment was only slightly better than in the upper-income group. Since the middle-income group evidently preferred to be identified with the upper-income group, Bank A realized that these two areas needed the greatest attention. Marketing efforts in these directions were the chief lesson learned from this phase of the survey.

DEMAND ACCOUNTS

A survey was not conducted on special checking accounts because the dollar attainment was not deemed significant enough. It could be done, however, and if so two factors can be applied. First, the dollar average here will not show the variation that is experienced in savings or regular demand, so that a more uniform treatment can be applied. Second, and of more positive influence, attainment versus potential in this field is a good indicator of convenience banking, and where growth is evident could provide a good clue to future expansion. If such a survey is to be undertaken, the same methodology and data would apply.

DEMAND POTENTIAL

To recapitulate, Bank A had approximately 4,400 demand accounts aggregating $4.7 million. The ledgers were run through with three colored pencils to indicate their categorization within the three economic areas mentioned. Once this had been done a 10 per cent sample was made within each category to determine averages and also via the hash-mark method within categories to obtain an account per family correlation. Again, only the accounts assigned to Office A were used in this exploratory sample. Of the 4,400, approximately 3,100 were domiciled in A, of which 1,900 were located in A via the colored pencil procedure.

Several comments are worthwhile here. The first is that about 40 per cent of the accounts maintained at Office A were actually located, by address, in communities other than A or B and were not subject to any pattern except perhaps the generalization that many were observably related to business now or previously located in A. The second is the obvious importance of the upper-income area both in numbers of accounts

Table 15

INDICATED DEMAND POTENTIAL

	Total Number	Average Balance	Indicated Total Balances
Lower Income	470	$ 310	$ 145,700
Middle Income	380	480	172,400
Upper Income	1,050	1,905	2,000,250
	1,900		$2,328,350

and in averages. Third, there is the matter of accounts per family. In the middle group there was almost no correlation to indicate that there was only one account per family if the families held regular checking accounts at all. In the lower-income group there was a small correlation estimated on the basis of the sample at approximately 1.1. In the upper-income group the indicated total potential of 650 families turned up over 1.6 accounts for the total number of families in the area. Bank A had always been under the impression that it was not getting its full share of this upper-income business—that the balances were going to the larger banks in the distant metropolitan areas. The knowledge gained through this survey was sobering but also brought strong realization of the unpredictability of balances from upper-income groups.

The knowledge gained thus far provided the basis for a simple check on business held in Office B. Community B more closely approximates that of the middle-income group in A than any other, it being largely a newer community of houses in the $20,000–$30,000 range. This check was performed by using numbers of accounts in B and middle-income averages as follows:

	Number of Accounts	Middle Average	Indicated Totals	Actual Totals
Savings	800	585	468,000	850,000
Demand (Regular)	1,300	480	624,000	900,000

Community B would appear to be somewhat more mature than the middle-income sector of A which is verified by the average age and length of occupancy of its residents. Consequently, the true averages for B should be raised somewhat. On the other hand, B has some business not domiciled in B proper, although far less than was the case with A. This was not studied separately although it could be done rather easily by the methods already described.

THE USE OF KNOWLEDGE

Thus far practically all of the do-it-yourself description has dealt with internal analysis of business already obtained within the immediate communities where the bank has its offices. This was intended as a means of indicating the various ways and degrees to which self-analysis can be applied. What has been learned? Bank A has learned several significant facts which are unique to its own situation. These may be summarized as follows:

1. Lower-income savings are significant but are not a growth element.
2. Upper-income penetration has been excellent, but indeterminate in relation to an unknown total potential.
3. The newer middle-income areas are not particularly fertile at present, but are areas of growth both in numbers and in average balances.
4. A substantial amount of checking business lies outside the immediate trade areas but is in some way related to those trade areas—especially the upper-income section.

These and many more facts will be brought to light by the process of self-analysis. They are the guideposts for managerial decision.

External Application

Bank A can now turn to the possibility of branches. It has been interested in the town some three miles to the southeast of B, a town for which B has a clear distance advantage but yet a town in which selective interview revealed a valence in other directions. Office B's ledgers were marked for business located in Town C to the southeast. The totals revealed were some 110 demand accounts, 80 savings accounts, and 140 special checking accounts in a town with an estimated population of 4,200, or some 1,100 families. Observable housing and income conditions closely approximated those in Town B. Using revised averages based on the experience in B and in the middle-income sector of A, the bank made the computations given in Table 16.

Table 16

BRANCH CONSIDERATION

	Average Balance	Total Potential	Probable Attainment	Now Held Balances	Probable Balances
Savings	$650	1,000	400	$ 52,000	$280,000
Demand	500	650	300	55,000	150,000
Special	180	250	175	25,000	31,500
				$132,000	$461,500

As can be seen, Town C, on the basis of these computations, could reasonably be expected to add some $300,000 to deposits if a branch were established there. This amount cooled the ardor of several directors who had felt that the town represented a gold mine of further expansion. It is this kind of concrete knowledge which self-analysis can provide if consistently pursued. There are mainly two things: (1) it provides a realistic understanding of average balances within homogeneous economic communities and (2) more importantly perhaps, it forces a more realistic appraisal of probable attainment within a given trade area even in the absence of competition.

An Incomplete Study

This do-it-yourself example of one bank's circumstances has probably raised more questions than it has answered. Although not too satisfying, this was the intention. Self-analysis is and should be a unique matter with each institution and the degree of investigation in each area should be determined by that bank's increasing knowledge as it pursues the several possible steps. Such an example cannot be satisfying but it is useful if it is either irritating or intriguing enough to cause others to make similar efforts. There is no substitute for individual examination in this business.

X

Conclusions

There is much left to say and the problem here, as it has been throughout, is one of choosing the important points in attempting to establish a few useful guideposts for banking expansion. There is a temptation to discuss over-all trends, for this is like speculating on a pennant race before any of the season's games have been played. But the trends are formed by the games as they are played, that is, moving from the specific to the general, and that is the procedure followed here. Comments will be made in sequence on individual bank analysis, expansion, and lastly over-all trends.

But first things first and unquestionably the greatest lesson learned in this effort should be restated now since it must be kept in mind in weighing the usefulness of the subequent comments. Simply, *each situation is unique.*

INDIVIDUAL BANK ANALYSIS

The obvious first step is to examine and understand the nature of the bank's deposits. When these categories of deposits are geographically plotted and reconsidered on the basis of small, economically homogeneous subareas, the shape of the trade area will become known and so will the true family or spending unit potential within those areas. Further, historical comparisons are not only possible but extremely useful especially to show where a bank may be living on an old and declining base. In any event, the primary lesson to be learned is the necessity for such understanding even if only the better to maintain the status quo. It is to be noted that no comments have been made on the whys of competitive attraction. It has been felt that to do so would direct attention away from the basic necessity for quantitative analysis. Knowledge of quantitative attainment by type and area can provide the background for such competitive efforts. The basic message to the individual bank is really that simple, though much could be said about sampling techniques and methods of statistical correlation, and a few of the simpler ones were described in the preceding chapter. Basically it is a matter of applying arithmetic and ingenuity to the unique data which only the individual bank possesses.

EXPANSION ANALYSIS

The consideration of possible expansion offensively, defensively, or in combination follows directly from present analysis. The character of already held business in the proposed area and in adjacent areas will provide the best possible measure for the unit size of business that can be obtained. The number of accounts to be obtained is entirely another matter, however. Here, again, internal analysis of actual versus potential will have a realistic influence. This conservative view must be combined with the best possible sampling of the proposed area. If the new subarea has no banking facility and the proposed location is in concert with a true convenience shopping locus, then a figure of 40 per cent of total potential within the area of demonstrated valence is probably a safe figure. If the proposed location is a convenience standoff with an existing institution, no allowance [1] should be made for competitive displacement. This brings up an extremely important aspect of expansion planning. Unless a new location is being planned for purely defensive reasons, there must be indication of future growth within the new trade area. It is important to recall in the case of successful new Bank G that, although the bank grew some $6 million in two years, its conservative competitor enjoyed approximately the same increase. In none of the cases reviewed was there an instance in which a new office grew at the expense of a competitor unless there was a clear-cut locational advantage. The absence of discernible growth was the reason for the charter refusal in Case J and for the negative branch decision in Case F. There have been many such instances where branches have been built in which management will admit the results only privately, if then.

The next major point concerning expansion planning is the necessity for a location which is part of a community trade center of either established or truly predictable drawing power. The two shopping center cases, A and B, are significant examples of what is hoped for versus what can happen. As a generalization a bank should beware of small new shopping centers unless there is both defensive justification and indicated growth in the area.

This leads to the exception to the rule of an established trading center—the strategic access case. Here, again, although the aim may be an offensive one, such a move is usually well based on defensive servicing of existing business.

What general conclusions on expansion planning? There would appear to be two: (1) banking growth in new locations must come from growth in those new areas rather than from established banking wealth and (2) there will be a great deal more physical expansion to defend existing business. It must be remembered that existing business can also be growth business as the customers and their banking assets mature. Probably there will be more semidefensive than pure expansion in the years ahead.

As for "defensive expansion," the term itself is somewhat redundant. More probably this activity should be called "modernization" and it will represent an area toward which many banks will focus their attention in the next several years. One main point is evident here: constructing an edifice will not, per se, improve the prospects of a given bank. If the bank's business is of such a nature that physical convenience is not the major determinant, an imposing building may be in order. Otherwise any money spent on downtown locations should be aimed at the two objectives of better access and better internal convenience for customers. As the trend of urban redevelopment grows, many banks will be offered the opportunity of providing a significant element of the new construction. It is human nature to be tempted but capital dollars entirely disproportionate to the probable deposit increase are at stake. Let the buyer beware.

It is suggested that two lesser cost alternatives deserve careful consideration in dealing with the modern service problem. These are the parking lot and the limited-service facility. Results are difficult to measure but so are the results of a new main office building, and in the two cases suggested here the investment is substantially less. To repeat, if you know your market, these decisions will be easier to reach.

COMMENTS ON DEPOSITS

The big thing for nearly all banks to remember is that the overwhelming portion of a bank's business is retail business and that even in the commercial category convenience is paramount. Several other comments are pertinent. Commercial and industrial business is small enough in numbers of accounts but big enough and variable enough in dollars to warrant individual review in any planning situation. A possible exception is the categorization of certain types of uniform business such as the local barbershop. This is not true even of small businesses where inventories can tie up proportionately large amounts of the enterprise's capital. The variation in balances from, say, automobile service stations can be large.

In the retail area several enlightening things have been learned. Special checking accounts are rather homogeneous in nature, averaging nationally between $100 and $200. Such a service is a necessity for successful marketing today, for the near-banking institutions are providing a parallel service through the sale of money orders. In the absence of undue competitive pressure the fees for this service should cover its cost, with the small balances providing a modest profit. From the point of view of convenience determination of a trade area, special checking account locations probably provide the best geographic plot, but the same plot should not be presumed to hold entirely true for the other deposit categories.

Savings accounts show some homogeneity but only for small economically homogeneous areas. The variation in characteristics between the lower- and middle-income savers in the do-it-yourself bank shows this and so does the average account realized in shopping center Case B. Age and occupational character mean more than income in the determination of average savings account balances.

It is frequently said that the value in savings account business is that it is cumulative and tends automatically to growth. It is also frequently said that savings business is an old business built upon the immigration influx which reached its peak some fifty years ago. Savings business is indeed cumulative but it cuts both ways. The lower-income savings attainment of the do-it-yourself bank in all probability will be a declining one as the older families pass on. This is a real problem for some savings institutions in old communities. Heirs are usually little interested in letting their inheritances remain on deposit. The degree of savings cumulation is interestingly revealed by an aggregate review of the savings held in New York City and in Elizabeth, New Jersey.[2] In New York City it was estimated that the average savings family (not including nonsavers) had an average of 3.0 accounts per family, with total balances of

$4,700. In Elizabeth the number of accounts was about the same and the family total approximated $5,000. Unquestionably much of this is older business which will atrophy.

But the savings business need not be considered a dying business. Indeed in terms of contact with the general public it is the most important single category today. Evidence of this and evidence that it need not be a dying business are provided (Table 17) by the most recent compilations on the overall savings market.

Table 17

STATISTICS ON THE SAVINGS MARKET[3]

	Commercial Banks	Savings Banks	Savings & Loan Associations	Credit Unions
Numbers of Savers	52,800,000	22,276,000	24,353,000	10,539,000
Savers per Office	2,336	23,577	3,337	561
Average Account	$835	$1,527	$1,967	$358

Several matters are striking and worthy of the pondering of those in the respective fields. The stake of the commercial banks is huge in terms of numbers of customers and the account density balance would appear to be good. Further, the commercial bank position is understated since the figures are three years older than those of the other types of institutions. The aggregate savings figure used here for commercial banks is approximately $44 billion. The reported total at year-end 1958 was $60 million. Therefore gains have been made but an undetermined portion of those gains represents time deposits of foreign central banks and other institutions which are not true savers.

The savings banks' base of operations is appallingly narrow and it is evidently a problem of which the banks are aware.

The success of the savings and loan industry is striking in two ways: (1) they seem to have a good base in terms of savers per office and (2) they give the lie to the contention that savings is an old business, since practically all of their business is a postwar phenomenon. The average account size is further evidence that savings need not be an old business.

As to credit unions, two comments are worthwhile: (1) their numerical growth has been far greater than any of the other categories and certainly represents a rising trend. The average account size here is probably substantially understated as it is understood that many members keep only a nominal balance in exchange for a check-cashing privilege. (2) Although small as units, credit unions apparently provide a stronger feeling of true mutuality than do the other mutual institutions. This is understandable for small units and their future growth will be an important trend to watch.

DEMAND DEPOSITS

This is the area that most persistently defies analysis. It is also for commercial banks the area of greatest importance. The feeling has been gained that perhaps individual demand deposits should be considered at two levels, the consistent and the irrational. By consistent it is meant that some generalizations can probably be made as to normal deposits in relation to age, income, and occupation and that this will be a worthwhile field for further study. The irrational portion consists of those overlarge balances which some few individuals maintain and which are well in excess of reasonable need. It is impossible to estimate these moneys—every bank has some and they unquestionably distort the averages. One thing is certain, such distortions should be deleted from any expansion planning averages. In fact, a review of self-analysis to adjust for this phenomenon would be in order for each bank. Once this is done, some of the mystery of this field will have been eliminated.

THE AGGREGATE VIEW

The comments in this final section cover three areas of over-all importance for the future. They are not of the who-will-win-the-pennant type, but rather of what kind of shape will the league be in when the season is over. Although no one unit can determine this, the aggregate of individual efforts will.

Monetary Policy and the Banking Industry

From all that can be seen we will continue to operate under a policy of countercyclical monetary persuasion actuated by the Federal Reserve Board. As such, the banking and near-banking industries will serve as the flexible pipeline through which the economy will alternately be fed and starved in the search for business stability. This means changes in the prices of the banking industry's products to an extent unthinkable in any other major field. This situation is further hardened by the circumstances of international trade, wherein for the first time since World War I the United States is competing economically on a truly level basis against other economies which can match us in quality, design, and above all, cost. Awareness of this peculiar but necessary position should permeate any and all plans for banking expansion.

Changing Markets

The new focus of monetary policy has other meanings for banking. Public awareness of the value of deposited money is at an all-time high and is likely to increase rather than diminish. Consequently, it may well be that banking will have to look more in the direction of fees as a source of future earnings. It also may well be that banking will have to provide new services to maintain and improve its markets. In-plant banking has been mentioned, areas of customer accounting services are widening steadily, and it is altogether possible that some form of hybrid checking account-savings account-mutual fund may be the marketing package of the future. Banks will need ingenuity and flexibility.

Saturation

Lastly there is the problem of possible overbanking as the several components of banking and near banking vie for the market. It is to be hoped that self-knowledge of the type suggested here will enable each unit to appraise its physical expansion possibilities more objectively. If self-objectivity is not forthcoming, the result, via some rough experience, will be unified supervision over all aspects of banking. Success comes through flexibility and sound expansion is the way to ensure that flexibility.

Appendix I

Revised January 1961

SUMMARY OF INFORMATION WHICH SHOULD BE MADE
AVAILABLE TO THE EXAMINER WHEN HE CONDUCTS AN
INVESTIGATION IN CONNECTION WITH A PROPOSED BRANCH

(1) The exact address of proposed branch—number and street, city or town, and county. If a definite location has not been settled, then the approximate location within a reasonable area should be given, i.e., in the vicinity of the intersection of _____ Avenue and _____ Street, and the radius of the vicinity in feet from that point.

(2) Give population of Head Office as of last census and a present estimate.

(3) Give population of city in which the proposed branch is to be located as of last census and a present estimate.

(4) (a) Give estimated population of immediate area which the branch will serve.

    (b) State approximate geographic boundaries of the service area.

    (c) This area extends from the branch location approximately _____ miles north; _____ miles east; _____ miles south; and _____ miles west.

    (Area should be outlined on the maps, and on any aerial photograph provided.)

(5) Describe the types of banking service the branch will offer; list the major types of demands for loans; also state whether the branch will serve to relieve overcrowded lobby or working conditions in the Head Office or certain branches, or will serve as an adjunct to any such office or branches.

Information given should make clear the reasons why the bank desires to establish the proposed branch.

(6) State distance and geographical direction of the Head Office from proposed branch.

(7) Provide the following information with respect to applicant's existing branches and any approved branches that are as yet unopened, located within a five-mile radius of proposed branch (one or two miles in large cities). Describe any geographical barriers.

Names and Addresses	If opened within five years—Date Established	Total Deposits Loans	Distance by road miles and direction from proposed branch

NOTE: If deposits and loans are not segregated, provide information based upon the most recent tabulations or estimates indicating dates thereof and by (E) if estimated.

(8) Provide a list of names and addresses of competitor banks and branches, including any known approved but unopened, located within a five-mile radius of the proposed branch (one- or two-mile radius in large cities).

(9) Provide handy-sized duplicate maps of the city or area appropriately labeled to show the location of the proposed branch and the names and locations of all banks and branches listed at (7) and (8) above, a scale of miles, and compass points. Current aerial photographs of reasonable coverage including the expected service area are helpful, and if available to the applicant, duplicate photographs labeled to correspond with the maps should also be provided, with the date made noted on the reverse side. The geographical boundaries of the expected service area of the proposed branch should be outlined on the maps, and on any aerial photographs provided.

(10) Provide a copy of any survey made preliminary to filing the bank's application for the proposed branch. Comment on the economic character of the area to be served. That is, if the area is largely residential, state whether the homes are generally owner-occupied, the extent of housing development, type, quality, price level, average age, number of unsold new homes, and prospects for continued or further development. If the area is primarily industrial or business, state the number and general types of business, and in cases of principal employers, give the name of each company or firm, number of employees, and payrolls, and comment on the consistency of employment and any special skills required. If the proposed branch is to be located in a shopping center, that center should be described fully as to the extent plans for construction and financing have progressed, if construction is not yet completed. State the number of units, size as to total land and building areas, number of individual automobile parking spaces, accessibility to surrounding communities, the extent to which signed leases have been obtained, the names of principal

lessees, and provide some information as to their financial responsibility if they are not nationally known reputable concerns. Provide information to show any growth record over an appropriate period of time, or growth prospects such as population trends, new businesses recently established or expected, etc. Also discuss the traffic pattern, the street and road facilities, and their adequacy. Any additional information which the applicant believes would be helpful in describing the economic character and prospects of the area to be served should be provided.

(11) Provide estimates of deposits and loans now held in the Head Office or other branches originating in the area to be served by proposed branch; also estimates of deposits and loans which the proposed branch may hold at the end of one year's operations and which the proposed branch may hold at the end of three years' operations.

(12) (a) If the proposed branch is not intended primarily to better serve the bank's existing customers, what period of time will be required to place the operations of the branch on a profitable basis?

(b) To what extent will the proposed branch enable the bank to serve more efficiently and thereby protect existing business?

(13) Give the following information regarding branch banking house and equipment as it applies:

(a) If to be purchased, the separate costs of land, building, furniture and fixtures, and vault.

(b) If to be leased, describe the quarters, and give terms in brief.

(c) Dimensions of lot.

(d) Dimensions of building. Numbers of stories above and below ground level.

(e) Square feet of floor area the building will contain; square feet of area the bank will occupy; respective numbers of inside tellers' windows and drive-in windows in the building; the numbers of separate walk-up and drive-in tellers' islands or pods, if any, and the number of individual automobile parking spaces to be provided or to be made available for the bank's use. If separate walk-up or drive-in tellers' islands or pods are to be used, describe the type of connection (common roof, tunnel, passageway, pneumatic tube, etc.) that will be used to integrate them into a single branch operation. Provide a sketch of lot showing locations of buildings, driveways and parking areas, and types of connections, if any.

(f) If property is to be purchased or leased from a director, officer, or large shareholder, state name.

(g) Give date of option to purchase or lease, if any, and state expiration date and provisions for renewal.

(h) If new construction, give approximate dates it will be started and completed.

(i) If a temporary location is to be occupied, so state, giving exact address, distance and direction from permanent location, and the estimated period of time it will be occupied.

(j) Give estimated date that branch can be placed in operation following approval. If beyond six months, give reason for delay.

(k) If steps have not been taken to secure quarters for the proposed branch, what are bank's plans?

Appendix II

1. Supply five copies of all material.
2. The exact address of proposed bank showing street and number as well as city and county. If a definite location has not been settled, the approximate location within a reasonable area should be given.
3. Proposed bank title, naming three in order of preference.
4. Proposed initial capital structure showing capital, surplus, undivided profits, number of shares, par value, and sales price.
5. The following data should be supplied by each organizer, proposed director and officer.

   Name

   Home address

   Length of residence in community

   Age

   Marital status giving number of Dependents

   State place of birth and indicate whether or not a citizen of U.S., if not native born give date of naturalization.

   If presently indebted state amount and type of borrowing and from whom borrowing, if not indebted state where banking business is conducted.

   Will full time be devoted to bank?

   If you have had previous banking experience give name of bank, position held and dates of service.

Occupational background (excluding above) giving name and location of firm, type of business, position held and length of service, this to include past as well as present.

If you have ever been bankrupt, discharged by an employer or convicted of a crime, give details.

Par Value of proposed stock subscription.

6. Give the population of city, town or village in which proposed bank is to be located, at last census and the present estimate.

7. Estimated population of the area to be served, as well as the approximate radius of this area. This to be shown on map required under question #24.

8. Describe the approximate geographical boundaries of the service area of the proposed bank and submit information on the economic character of the area, such as wealth characteristics, resident ownership, shopping center, industrial establishments, number and general type of business houses, employment characteristics of residents, payrolls, prospective population and business growth and so forth. Name principal businesses and industries, with information as to approximate number of people employed by each. If available, give approximate annual dollar volume of business and gross annual payrolls. Indicate relative stability and trends of these businesses over past ten (10) years and discuss future prospects.

9. Financial position of city, town, village, school districts and county. Discuss tax collections, showing total levy, percentage collected and arrears, etc.

10. List names and addresses of competitor banks, branches and other financial institutions, within a five mile radius (2–3 miles in large cities), showing capital structure, deposit and loan totals for each (if available) and the distance and direction of each from the location of proposed bank. (See #24.)

11. If no bank in community, where is banking business conducted by residents?

12. Past banking history of community.

13. Information to support the opinion that there is a public need for the proposed bank, including requests by local people.

14. What competitive effect is the proposed bank expected to create?

15. Give estimates of the volume of total deposits, showing the amount of public funds included in total, and total loans expected at the end of the first year of operations, second and third year.

16. List the major types of loaning demands proposed bank expects to serve.

17. Projected earnings and expenses:

Income	1st Year	2nd Year	3rd Year
Int. on loans			
Int. on Investments			
Other Income (Service Charges etc.)			
Total	———	———	———

Expenses
  Salaries
  Rent—Ins.
  Interest
  Taxes
  Other Expenses
               Total   _____   _____   _____
Net Profit or Loss   _____   _____   _____

18. Proposed ownership of stock, is it to be widely distributed or closely held? Amounts to be taken by organizers, proposed directors, officers and their families.

19. Physical description of quarters to be occupied by the proposed bank, showing any contemplated drive-in and parking arrangements.

20. If property is to be purchased give estimated cost. Is it presently owned by an organizer or proposed director or officer? Give name and address of owner.

21. If to be leased; give terms of lease and estimated cost of improvements to lessee.

22. Description of vault, furniture, fixtures and equipment for the proposed bank, along with a projection of their costs. If complete housing plans have not been formulated, limits should be set on expected investment in building, leasehold improvements, furniture, fixtures and equipment.

23. What plans have been made to obtain fidelity insurance covering all individuals authorized to collect, receive, or deposit funds from stock subscriptions?

24. Five maps should be provided on which are clearly indicated and identified the location of proposed bank and all other banking facilities and financial institutions within a five mile radius (2–3 miles in large cities) of the proposed bank.

25. Will bank acquire at least minimum amount of Fidelity insurance based on A.B.A. schedule?

Appendix III

SUMMARY OF VARIATIONS
STATE VS. NATIONAL BANK CHARTERS

Federal Reserve Membership

All national banks are members of the Federal Reserve System, but such membership is optional with state banks. If a state bank joins, it is, generally speaking, subject to the laws affecting national banks with respect to capital, reserves, branch banking, loans, investments, and interlocking personnel, each of which is discussed here.

Deposit Insurance

National banks and state Federal Reserve member banks are insured by the Federal Deposit Insurance Corporation, but such insurance is optional to nonmember state banks.[1] Nonmember insured banks are not subject to the statutes referred to below relating to capital and branches; however, the Federal Deposit Insurance Corporation gives consideration to capital and surplus in passing on the application of a nonmember state bank for insurance,[2] and no branch can be established without its consent.[3]

Capital and Surplus

The minimum capital and surplus requirements for national banks, as set forth in 12 U.S.C. Section 51, are in general greater than those for nonmember state banks.[4]

Reserves

The reserve requirements for national banks and state member banks are in general higher than those for nonmember state banks.[5] The required reserves of national and state member banks must be kept in a Federal Reserve bank and do not bear interest. Set forth in Paton *Supplement*, "Deposits," Section 25 is a compilation of state statutes relating to reserves of nonmember state banks.

Branch Banking
Generally speaking, a national bank has the same right to establish branches as it would if it were a state bank, except that there are special requirements as to capital and the approval of the Comptroller of the Currency is required.[6] State laws with respect to branch banking are summarized in the *Federal Reserve Bulletin* of October, 1939, and again in the July, 1950, issue.

Loans and Investments
Federal laws comprehensively regulate national bank loans and investments.[7] Most state regulations are less comprehensive.[8] Areas in which there are liable to be differences between the permitted activities of state banks, member banks, and national banks are the following: loans to officers and employees, the limitation on loans to a single borrower, the types of securities in which it may invest, and the requirements with respect to real estate loans.

Interlocking Personnel
Section 8 of the Clayton Act prohibits a director, officer, or employee of a member bank from serving in a similar capacity with another commercial bank when the member bank and the other bank have offices in the same community.[9] Nonmember state banks are not prohibited by federal law, however, from such interlocking relationships, and there is little state legislation on this subject.[10]

Stockholder Liability
Stockholders in national banks are, in nearly all cases, no longer subject to double liability; state statutes frequently still provide for it.[11]

Taxation
National banks are exempt from certain types of state taxation.[12]

Appendix IV

CENSUS DATA AVAILABLE FOR BANKING MARKET RESEARCH

This table summarizes the data of more importance to banking. Greater details are available; for example, age by sex, marital status, etc.

	COUNTIES	MINOR CIVIL DIVISIONS	WARDS AND ASSEMBLY DISTRICTS	METROPOLITAN AREAS	URBANIZED AREAS	URBAN PLACES 10,000 OR MORE	URBAN PLACES 2,500 TO 10,000	PLACES 1,000 TO 2,500
POPULATION:								
Totals	Yes	Yes	Some Areas[1]	Yes	Yes	Yes	Yes	Yes
Characteristics								
Age	Yes	Yes	No	Yes	Yes	Yes	Yes	Yes
No. over 65	Yes	No	No	Yes	Yes	Yes	Yes	Yes
No. Foreign Born	Yes	No	No	Yes	Yes	Yes	Yes	Yes
No. Nonwhite	Yes	Yes	No	Yes	Yes	Yes	Yes	Yes
Employment Status	Yes	No	No	Yes	Yes	Yes	Yes	No
Occupation Status	Yes	No	No	Yes	Yes	Yes	Yes	No
Income	Yes	No	No	Yes	Yes	Yes	Yes	No
Families	Yes	Yes[2]	No	Yes	Yes	Yes	Yes	Yes
Schooling	Yes	No	No	Yes	Yes	Yes	Yes	No

SPECIALIZED
CENSUS REPORTS:

Housing	Yes	No	No	**Yes**	Yes	Yes	Yes	No
Block Statistics	No	No	No	**Yes³**	Yes³	No	No	No
Census Tracts	No	No	No	**Yes**	Yes	No	No	No
Census of Business:								
Retail Trade	Yes	No	No	**Yes**	Yes	Yes	Yes	No
Wholesale Trade	Yes	No	No	**Yes**	Yes	Yes	Yes	No
Selected Services	Yes	No	No	**Yes**	Yes	Yes	Yes	No

1 Data by wards or assembly districts are only available for those political divisions so subdivided.
2 Although the number of families is not given for Minor Civil Divisions, the 1960 census does list the number of households in this category, from which the number of families can be accurately estimated.
3 Block statistics are available for most cities of 50,000 or more.

EXPLANATIONS OF CENSUS TERMS
Geographical Divisions

Minor Civil Divisions—A general term indicating the primary political units into which counties are divided. These are towns, townships, boroughs, etc.

Metropolitan Area—A county or group of contiguous counties which contain at least one city of 50,000 or more. In New England only part of a county may be included. Contiguous counties are included if they are essentially metropolitan in character and integrated with the city. The criteria for being metropolitan in character relate primarily to employment patterns and the concentrations of the workers and their dependents.

Urbanized Area—An area containing at least one city of 50,000 or more plus a thickly settled urban fringe. The area included is determined by the pattern of urban growth and not by civil division. In general it is the thickly settled urban core of the standard metropolitan area.

Urban Places—A concentration of population regardless of civil divisions. It includes all places of 2,500 or more. Those under 2,500 are termed "places." Data for places under 1,000 are given only under the heading of Minor Civil Divisions.

Population Characteristics

Foreign Born—Country of birth.

Employment—Figures on the total labor force, a breakdown by sex, numbers unemployed, major occupation groupings, and major industry groupings. Greater detail is available for metropolitan areas and cities of 100,000 or more.

Income—The median, or mid-point, income figures are indicated. Figures are for families, and families plus unrelated individuals. The total number is broken into classes of various income ranges. A family is a group of two or more persons related by blood, marriage, or adoption and living together.

Schooling—Numbers enrolled in school by ages and median school years completed for those over 25.

Occupation—Detailed occupation figures are available for standard metropolitan areas and for cities of 100,000 or more. More detailed data as to income by job and sex, racial breakdowns in occupations, ages of employed persons by occupations, etc., are available only for the major metropolitan areas.

Specialized Census Reports

Housing—Detailed reports on housing characteristics are available for all places of over 10,000. They include values of structures, rentals, heating facilities, sanitary facilities, etc. Less detail is available for places of between 2,500 and 10,000 population.

Block Statistics—These are issued for most cities of over 50,000. They indicate housing and tenancy characteristics for each city block.

Census Tracts—An information breakdown containing all population characteristics by small sections of 175 cities and their adjacent areas. Unpublished
data can be obtained from the Bureau of the Census at nominal cost for
subdivisions of the Census Tracts.

Census of Business Reports—These reports are issued every four years and divided into three categories: retail trade, wholsale trade, and selected
services. The latest reports were issued for 1958. They indicate employment, number of enterprises, payrolls, and sales, by both total and kind of
business groupings. More detail is available for the major business areas.

Appendix V

Tables Based on Data of Federal Reserve Board

SIZE OF LIQUID ASSET HOLDINGS—OCCUPATION GROUPS—1950
PERCENT OF EACH GROUP—AMOUNT OF CHECKING ACCOUNTS HELD

CHECKING ACCOUNT AMOUNT	PROFESSIONAL	MANAGEMENT AND SELF-EMPLOYED	CLERICAL & SALES	SKILLED & SEMI-SKILLED	RETIRED
Zero	29	27	52	74	60
$1–$499	41	37	34	26	14
$500–$1,999	19	20	9	4	15
$2,000 and over	11	16	5	6	11
	100%	100%	100%	100%	100%

SAVINGS ACCOUNTS HELD

	PROFESSIONAL	MANAGEMENT AND SELF-EMPLOYED	CLERICAL & SALES	SKILLED & SEMI-SKILLED	RETIRED
Zero	43	54	42	54	58
$1–$499	18	14	29	22	16
$500–$1,999	21	16	17	15	15
$2,000 and over	18	16	12	9	11
	100%	100%	100%	100%	100%

MEDIAN LIQUID HOLDINGS WITHIN INCOME GROUPS

INCOME GROUP	HOLDINGS	INCOME GROUP	HOLDINGS
$1,000	$ 0	$3,000–$3,999	$ 350
$1,000–$1,999	10	$4,000–$4,999	500
$2,000–$2,999	160	$5,000–$7,499	1,130
		$7,500 and over	4,270

SAVERS WITHIN INCOME AND OCCUPATIONAL GROUPS UNDER STANDARD AND ALTERNATIVE DEFINITIONS OF SAVING, 1950

(As a percentage of spending units within group)

GROUPS OF SPENDING UNITS	AMOUNTS SAVED									
	ALL POSITIVE SAVERS		$1,000 & OVER		$500–$999		$200–$499		$1–$199	
	STAND- ARD	ALTER- NATIVE	STAND- ARD	ALTER- NATIVE	STAND- ARD	ALTER- NATIVE	STAND- ARD	ALTER- NATIVE	STAND- ARD	ALTER- NATIVE
All Spending Units	61	62	15	16	12	13	14	15	20	18
By Income before taxes: *										
Under $1,000	34	28	†	†	†	†	7	5	27	23
$1,000–$1,999	53	50	2	1	6	7	15	17	30	25
$2,000–$2,999	59	61	7	8	12	13	16	16	24	25
$3,000–$3,999	67	70	11	12	17	16	20	23	19	19
$4,000–$4,999	69	72	20	19	18	23	17	16	14	14
$5,000–$7,499	75	81	37	37	19	23	10	13	9	8
$7,500 and over	87	86	73	74	6	7	6	4	2	1
By occupation of head of unit.‡										
Professional & semi-professional	65	68	27	24	13	18	12	14	12	12
Managerial & self-employed	73	73	39	38	13	17	10	9	10	9
Clerical & sales	67	72	14	18	12	11	21	22	22	21
Skilled & semi-skilled	65	69	10	10	17	18	16	19	22	22
Unskilled & service	52	55	7	7	10	11	12	15	23	22
Farm operator	60	62	24	25	12	11	10	14	16	12
Retired	45	32	6	5	2	5	7	3	30	19

* Excludes spending units for which income was not ascertained.
† No cases reported or less than one-half of 1%.
‡ Excludes spending units for which occupation of head was not ascertained and also spending units headed by housewives, students, unemployed persons, and protective service workers.

TYPE AND SIZE OF SELECTED LIQUID ASSET HOLDINGS WITHIN INCOME GROUPS

(Percentage Distribution of Spending Units)

TYPE & SIZE OF HOLDING	MONEY INCOME BEFORE TAXES IN 1957								
	Under $1,000	$1,000– $1,199	$2,000– $2,999	$3,000– $3,999	$4,000– $4,999	$5,000– $5,999	$6,000– $7,499	$7,500– $9,999	$10,000 AND OVER
Total Liquid Assets:									
Zero	62	50	37	32	25	16	10	2	1
$1–$199	12	14	14	20	22	24	21	15	4
$200–$499	6	12	13	12	20	16	17	16	9
$500–$999	4	6	12	10	7	11	16	15	15
$1,000–$1,999	5	3	7	9	10	12	14	19	17
$2,000–$4,999	7	8	9	11	13	12	12	21	21
$5,000–$9,999	2	5	4	3	1	6	6	8	15
$10,000 and over	1	2	5	3	4	3	4	4	19
All cases	100	100	100	100	100	100	100	100	100

Savings Accounts: *

Zero	81	69	64	55	48	37	34	28	29
$1–$199	5	6	9	10	17	19	19	15	10
$200–$499	3	7	7	9	12	13	13	12	9
$500–$999	2	4	8	5	5	8	9	12	9
$1,000–$1,999	3	3	3	9	7	8	12	12	10
$2,000 and over	5	11	10	11	12	14	13	22	32
All cases	100	100	100	100	100	100	100	100	100

Checking Accounts:

Zero	76	69	60	61	51	40	30	16	8
$1–$199	12	13	13	17	25	30	37	35	14
$200–$499	4	7	13	10	13	15	18	25	20
$500–$999	5	7	7	8	5	7	7	11	21
$1,000–$1,999	2	2	4	2	4	4	3	7	14
$2,000 and over	1	2	3	2	2	4	4	5	23
All cases	100	100	100	100	100	100	100	100	100

* Includes savings accounts in banks, postal savings, and shares in savings and loan associations and credit unions.

DISTRIBUTION OF POSITIVE AND NEGATIVE SAVERS ACCORDING TO RELATION OF SAVING TO INCOME BY INCOME GROUPS OF FAMILY UNITS, 1950

(Percentage distribution of family units within income groups)

POSITIVE AND NEGATIVE SAVERS	ALL GROUPS	FAMILY INCOME GROUPS *						
		UNDER $1,000	$1,000–$1,999	$2,000–$2,999	$3,000–$3,999	$4,000–$4,999	$5,000–$7,499	$7,500 AND OVER
POSITIVE SAVERS—total	61	30	51	55	66	66	74	86
Percentage of income saved:								
50 and over	4	3	5	4	2	2	3	10
30–49	8	3	5	8	8	8	11	16
20–29	9	4	4	7	7	12	13	15
10–19	17	6	13	13	20	20	23	23
1–9	23	14	24	23	29	24	23	22
ZERO SAVERS—total	6	31	12	6	†	1	†	†
NEGATIVE SAVERS—Total ‡	33	39	37	39	34	33	26	14
Dissaving as a percentage of income:								
1–9	12	5	11	15	16	16	13	7
10–24	10	4	13	12	11	12	8	5
25 and over	11	30	13	12	7	5	5	2
All cases	100	100	100	100	100	100	100	100
Number of cases	3,029	335	397	420	495	399	595	388

* Based on 1950 money income before taxes.

† No cases reported or less than one-half of 1 per cent.

‡ Family units with expenditures in excess of money income.

BLANK BANK
PRO FORMA
INITIAL EXPENDITURES
BALANCE SHEET AND INCOME ACCOUNT

Organization Expenses (legal fees, issuance of stock, advertising and other expenses incident to organization)	$20,000	
Furniture, Fixtures & Leasehold Improvements		
Vault Door, Safe Deposit Boxes, Money Chests, Vault Lining, Teller's Lockers, Night Depository, etc.		$ 32,000
Teller's cages (6)		13,200
Desks, chairs, misc. furniture		2,500
Machines		
4 adding machines @ $375	$1,500	
3 bookkeeping machines *	9,100	
1 savings bookkeeping	4,650	
1 Recordak	2,400	
1 check cancelling	350	
1 proof *	9,000	
3 typewriters	1,000	
		$28,000
Fixtures, coupon booths, lighting, plumbing, ventilation ducts, etc.†		30,000
Decorating, signs, carpeting		10,000
Total Furniture, Fixtures & Leasehold		$115,700
(to be capitalized; depreciation $5,750 per annum)		

EMPLOYEES

1 Manager	$ 9,000
1 Assistant Manager	6,000
2 Tellers	6,000
2 Bookkeepers	6,000
	$27,000

* May be available used.
† Air-conditioning expense may be higher.

BLANK BANK
PRO FORMA BALANCE SHEET AND INCOME ACCOUNT

(Immediate deposit level $900,000: $400,000 commercial, $500,000 directed. Attained deposit level at end of 1st year $1,500,000: $500,000 time, $500,000 regular commercial, $500,000 directed; average deposits available during year $1,200,000. Attained level 2nd year $2,500,000; average available 2nd year $2,000,000.)

ASSETS	END OF FIRST YEAR AMOUNT IN $	% OF TOTAL ASSETS	FIRST YEAR INCOME & EXPENSE INCOME†	ASSETS	END OF SECOND YEAR AMOUNT IN $	% OF TOTAL ASSETS	SECOND YEAR INCOME & EXPENSE INCOME†
Vault Cash	$ 55,000	3	—	Vault Cash	$ 84,000	3	—
Due from Banks	236,000	13	—	Due from Banks	375,000	13	—
Total Nonearning	$ 291,000	16		Total Nonearning	$ 459,000	16	
Secondary Res.	$ 333,000	18	$ 5,000	Secondary Res.	$ 484,000	17	$ 7,100
Bond Inv. Acct.	420,000	23	9,200	Bond Inv. Acct.	597,000	21	14,800
Personal Loans	403,000	22	27,300	Personal Loans	710,000	25	63,300
Other Loans	146,000	8	4,800	Other Loans	205,950	7	9,800
Mortgages	102,200	7	3,900	Mortgages	292,950	10	14,700
Total Earning	$1,404,200	78	Gross Inc. $50,200	Total Earning	$2,289,900	80	Gross Inc. $109,700
Furn., Fixt. & Lsehld. Imp.	$ 109,250	6		Furn., Fixt. & Lsehld. Imp.	$ 103,500	4	
Total Assets	$1,804,450	100		Total Assets	$2,852,400	100	

LIABILITIES & CAPITAL

		EXPENSES	
Capital	$ 100,000	Int. Time Dep.	$ 5,000
Surplus	150,000	Salaries	27,000
Undivided Pfts.	64,450	Rent	13,000
Demand Deposits	1,000,000	Operating Exp.	5,000
Time Deposits	500,000	Depreciation	5,750
		Organization Exp.	20,000
Total Liab. & Cap.	$1,804,450	Total Expense	$75,750
		Loss for Year	$25,550

LIABILITIES & CAPITAL

		EXPENSES	
Capital	$ 100,000	Int. Time Dep.	$ 15,000
Surplus	150,000	Salaries	33,000
Undivided Pfts.	102,400	Rent	13,000
Demand Deposits	1,500,000	Operating Exp.	5,000
Time Deposits	1,000,000	Depreciation	5,750
Total Liab. & Cap.	$2,852,400	Total Expense	$71,750
		Pre Tax Income	$37,950*

* Probably not subject to tax due to loss carry-forward.
† Income is based on the following averages for earning assets at rates of return indicated:

	% RATE OF RETURN	AVERAGE FOR 1ST YEAR	AVERAGE FOR 2ND YEAR
Secondary Reserves	1.5	$333,000	$473,000
Bond Inv. Acct.	2.5	370,000	592,000
Personal Loans	9.0	303,000	703,000
Other Loans	5.0	96,000	196,000
Mortgages	5.0	77,750	292,000

Appendix VII

FORM 82 *Application to be filed by an organizing bank for Federal Deposit Insurance.*

FORM 85 REVISED 5-1-52

Application to Establish a Branch

SAMPLE COPY

FEDERAL DEPOSIT INSURANCE CORPORATION
WASHINGTON, D. C.

SIRS:

The ...., hereinafter
       Name of Bank   Street Address   City or Town and State
referred to as the Applicant Bank, hereby makes application to the Federal Deposit Insurance Corporation for written
consent to establish a branch at ....
                                    Street Address

.... The Branch which the Applicant
    City or Town   County   State

Bank desires to establish is to be known at its proposed location as ...., is to be ....
                                          Exact Legal Title
distant from the main office of the Applicant Bank, and is hereafter referred to in this Application as the Proposed Branch.

The general character or type of business to be exercised by the Proposed Branch is as follows:

(Check all appropriate items)
( ) Commercial banking; ( ) Savings banking; ( ) Industrial banking; ( ) Trust business; ( ) Cash depository;
( ) Receiving deposits and cashing checks only; ( ) Others.

Specify...

It is understood that the Board of Directors of the Federal Deposit Insurance Corporation in applying the factors set out in Section 6 of the Federal Deposit Insurance Act to this Application, will consider it only with respect to the general character or type of business above stated and that the bank will not engage in any other business without the prior written consent of the Corporation.

The following are citations of State statutory provisions and regulations which govern the establishment, operation, and powers of the Proposed Branch:

We have, in connection with this Application, read the following provisions of the Federal Deposit Insurance Act which govern applications by State nonmember banks to establish a branch, namely:

"Sec. 3. (o) The term 'branch' includes any branch bank, branch office, branch agency, additional office, or any branch place of business located in any State of the United States or in any Territory of the United States, Puerto Rico, or the Virgin Islands at which deposits are received or checks paid or money lent."

"Sec. 18. (d) No State nonmember insured bank (except a District bank) shall establish and operate any new branch unless it shall have the prior written consent of the Corporation, ... The factors to be considered in granting or withholding the consent of the Corporation under this subsection shall be those enumerated in section 6 of this Act."

"Sec. 6. The factors . . . to be considered by the Board of Directors . . . shall be the following: The financial history and condition of the bank, the adequacy of its capital structure, its future earnings prospects, the general character of its management, the convenience and needs of the community to be served by the bank, and whether or not its corporate powers are consistent with the purposes of this Act."

In support of this Application, the following statements, representations, and information upon the several factors enumerated in Section 6 of the Federal Deposit Insurance Act are submitted for the purpose of inducing the Board of Directors of the Federal Deposit Insurance Corporation to grant its prior written consent to the establishment of the Proposed Branch:

1

FORM 66M REVISED 5-1-52

(1) FINANCIAL HISTORY AND CONDITION

The following is a statement of the assets and liabilities of the Applicant Bank as of the date of this Application:

The name and address of the main office and of each existing branch and the total amount of deposits arising as a result of the operation of the main office and of each existing branch as of the date of this Application are shown in the following schedule:

It is anticipated that a normal deposit volume of approximately $...will be obtained by the Proposed Branch within..months after its establishment.

The following is a detailed description of the premises to be occupied by the Proposed Branch. It includes name of owner and annual rental, if by lease; date of construction, original cost, price to be paid, and from whom acquired, if by purchase; or the estimated cost, if new construction.

*The Proposed Branch is to be established as a result of a merger or consolidation of the Applicant Bank with.....................
---, --
                              Name of Bank   City
---, or the purchase of assets from, and the assumption of liabilities of, said bank.
         State

There are attached copies of all (proposed) contracts and documents to be used in effecting said transaction together with a statement of the assets and liabilities of the merged or purchased bank. Other information essential to a full understanding of the transaction is as follows:

(2) ADEQUACY OF SURPLUS OR CAPITAL STRUCTURE

The surplus or capital structure of the Applicant Bank, as of the date of this Application, is as follows:

	Amount
Capital Debentures...................................(Retirable at $...)	
Surplus or Guaranty Fund..	
Undivided profits...	
Other segregations of the surplus or capital structure..	
Total Surplus or Capital Structure	

The surplus or capital requirements of State law relative to the operation of the Applicant Bank, the Proposed Branch, and other existing branches, as contemplated in this Application are as follows:

The Applicant Bank will at all times maintain, or provide satisfactory and effective means for attaining, an adequate total sound surplus or capital structure in relation to the true value of its assets.

*This paragraph need not be complied with, of course, unless the Proposed branch is established as a result of any of the transactions therein mentioned.

FORM 83 REVISED 5-1-52

(3) FUTURE EARNINGS PROSPECTS

There follows a statement of the current operating earnings and expenses of the Applicant Bank or its Predecessor Institution during the last calendar year or for the twelve month period ending ....; or, if the Applicant Bank has been recently organized and has no Predecessor Institution, there follows a pro forma statement of anticipated current operating earnings and expenses for the first twelve months following membership of Applicant Bank in the Federal Deposit Insurance Corporation:

Current Operating Earnings		*Current Operating Expenses*	
(a) Interest and discount on loans	————	(a) Interest on time and savings deposits . . .	————
(b) Interest and dividends on securities . . .	————	(b) Interest and discount on borrowings . . .	————
(c) Commissions, fees, and collection, exchange, and service charges	————	(c) Salaries and wages	————
		(d) Taxes (other than on net income)	————
(d) Other current operating earnings	————	(e) Other current operating expenses	————
Gross Current Operating Earnings	————	Total Current Operating Expenses	————

The following is an itemization of current operating expenses on a yearly basis which will result from the operation of the Proposed Branch:

It is the opinion of the undersigned that the operating earnings which will result from the operation of the Proposed Branch will be sufficiently in excess of the estimated current operating expenses listed above to justify the operation of the Proposed Branch.

(4) MANAGEMENT

The proposed members of the local advisory board (or local directors) and the proposed officers of the Proposed Branch are listed below with information in regard to each. Following the name of each of the proposed officers is a brief resume or outline of his past business or banking experience and other qualifications as well as a brief statement of his duties and responsibilities in connection with the operation of the Proposed Branch.

Name, address and occupation	Age	Title and duties	Net worth	Annual salary	Par value of stock owned Preferred Common

Officers of the Proposed Branch will have the following authority in connection with the granting of loans and discounts and extending credit:

A brief summary of the supervision and control which will be exercised by the officials of Applicant Bank over the activities of the Proposed Branch is as follows:

The Applicant Bank will at all times maintain sufficient surety bond coverage on its active officers and employees to conform with generally accepted banking practices.

FORM 82 REVISED 5-1-52

(5) CONVENIENCE AND NEEDS OF COMMUNITY

Existing banks and branches of banks located in same city or town as proposed Bank and existing banks and branches of banks located within a radius of twenty-five miles of proposed Bank are as follows:

Name of bank or branch	Location	Population	Approximate deposits	Distance from proposed bank

The approximate population of the town or city in which the proposed Bank will be located is... .....

The approximate population of the trade area to be served is ....

The principal industries of the community are:

Name	Type	Approximate number of employees	Approximate annual payroll	Approximate annual sales

The principal agricultural, mineral, and other products of the territory to be served are:

The approximate average annual value of the above products during the past three years is:

Other supporting information relative to the factor of convenience and needs of the community is as follows:

(6) CONSISTENCY OF CORPORATE POWERS

It is contemplated that the proposed Bank will have only such corporate powers as are granted to a State banking corporation under the following provisions of the State law:

It is expressly agreed that the Bank, while a member of the Federal Deposit Insurance Corporation, will not, except as incidental to the usual functions of a bank, guarantee mortgages, mortgage or other participation certificates, or real estate land titles or obligate itself under any contract of suretyship or guaranty.

There is attached hereto (if available) a copy of the proposed Articles of Incorporation or Association.

CERTIFICATE

The undersigned hereby certify, jointly and severally, that the statements contained in this Application are true to their best knowledge and belief, and that they are made for the purpose of inducing the Federal Deposit Insurance Corporation to accept the proposed Bank when organized as a member of the Federal Deposit Insurance Corporation.

Dated:..

Signed: Address:

--   ....

--   ....

--   ....

--   ....

INFORMATION FOR APPLICANT

1. Any prospective incorporator desiring to qualify his certificate may do so by attaching hereto any statement which may be required to make his certificate accurate.
2. Schedules or inserts may be attached to this Application wherever the space provided is insufficient. Such attached schedules or inserts are a part of this Application and likewise must be signed by the prospective incorporators. All schedules or inserts should preferably be on paper the same size as this page. Applications are to be securely bound at the top of the page.
3. This Application is to be executed in quadruplicate, three signed Applications to be forwarded to the Supervising Examiner of the Federal Deposit Insurance Corporation for the Federal Deposit Insurance District in which the proposed Bank is to be located and the other Application to be retained by the prospective incorporators.
4. If in any instance it is not clear as to what information is necessary to complete this Application, a letter to the Supervising Examiner of the Corporation for the District in which the Applicant is located will bring a prompt and informative reply.

4

FORM 85 REVISED 5-1-52

RESOLUTION OF BOARD OF DIRECTORS OF APPLICANT BANK

The Board of Directors of the Applicant Bank at a meeting duly called and held on...
adopted the following Resolution:
Date

"WHEREAS, it is the sense of this meeting that application should be made on behalf of this Bank to the Federal Deposit Insurance Corporation for written consent to establish a branch at..
(Street Address)

.... in accordance with the provisions
(City or Town)   (State)

of the Federal Deposit Insurance Act;

NOW, THEREFORE, IT IS RESOLVED, That the President or Vice-President and the Cashier or Secretary of this Bank are hereby authorized and directed to make application on behalf of this Bank to the Federal Deposit Insurance Corporation to establish a branch at...
(Street Address) (City or Town) (State)

and to submit to the Federal Deposit Insurance Corporation in connection therewith information on the several factors enumerated under Section 6 of the Federal Deposit Insurance Act for the purpose of inducing the Board of Directors of the Federal Deposit Insurance Corporation to grant its written consent to the establishment of a branch as indicated in this Resolution."

The above Resolution has not been rescinded or modified and has been duly entered on the minute book of the Applicant Bank.

It is requested that an Examiner of the Federal Deposit Insurance Corporation be assigned to conduct the necessary investigation or examination.

Date:................................ ....
(Name and Location of Applicant Bank)

(SEAL)   By:...
(President or Vice-President)

Attest:

....
(Cashier or Secretary)

CERTIFICATE OF DIRECTORS OF APPLICANT BANK

The undersigned, constituting a majority of the Directors of the Applicant Bank, do hereby certify and state, jointly and severally, that they have read this Application and all statements, representations, and information contained therein and that said statements, representations, and information are true and correct to the best of their knowledge and belief and are submitted for the purpose of inducing the Federal Deposit Insurance Corporation to grant its prior written consent to the establishment of a branch as provided in this Application.

Date:..

Signed: Address:

INFORMATION FOR APPLICANT

1. Any signing Director desiring to qualify his certificate may do so by attaching hereto any statement which may be required to make his certificate accurate.
2. Schedules or inserts may be attached to this Application wherever the space provided for certain information is insufficient. Such attached schedules or inserts are to be regarded as a part of this Application and must be signed by the Directors. All schedules or inserts should preferably be on paper the same size as this page. Applications are to be securely bound at the top of the page.
3. This Application is to be executed in quadruplicate, three signed Applications to be forwarded to the Supervising Examiner of the Federal Deposit Insurance Corporation for the Federal Deposit Insurance District in which the Applicant Bank is located and the other Application is to be retained in the files of the Applicant Bank.
4. If in any instance it is not clear as to what information is necessary to complete this Application, a letter to the Supervising Examiner of the Corporation for the District in which the Applicant Bank is located will bring a prompt and informative reply.

Appendix VIII

FORM 85M   *Application to be filed by a Mutual Savings Bank.*

FORM 85M REVISED 5-1-52

Application to Establish a Branch

(Mutual Savings Bank) *
SAMPLE

FEDERAL DEPOSIT INSURANCE CORPORATION
WASHINGTON, D. C.

SIRS:

The..., hereinafter
         Name of Bank   Street Address   City or Town and State
referred to as the Applicant Bank, hereby makes application to the Federal Deposit Insurance Corporation for written
consent to establish a branch at...
                                                               Street Address
.... The Branch which the Applicant
     City or Town   County   State
Bank desires to establish is to be known at its proposed location as ...., is to be ....
                                                      Exact Legal Title
distant from the main office of the Applicant Bank, and is hereafter referred to in this Application as the Proposed Branch.

The general character or type of business to be exercised by the Proposed Branch is as follows:

....

....
                                                                      (See Footnote*)

It is understood that the Board of Directors of the Federal Deposit Insurance Corporation in applying the factors set out
in Section 6 of the Federal Deposit Insurance Act to this Application, will consider it only with respect to the general
character or type of business above stated and that the bank will not engage in any other business without the prior
written consent of the Corporation.

The following are citations of State statutory provisions and regulations which govern the establishment, operation, and
powers of the Proposed Branch:

We have, in connection with this Application, read the following provisions of the Federal Deposit Insurance Act which
govern applications by State nonmember banks to establish a branch, namely:

"Sec. 3. (o)   The term 'branch' includes any branch bank, branch office, branch agency, additional office, or any
branch place of business located in any State of the United States or in any Territory of the United States, Puerto
Rico, or the Virgin Islands at which deposits are received or checks paid or money lent."

"Sec. 18. (d)   No State nonmember insured bank (except a District bank) shall establish and operate any new
branch unless it shall have the prior written consent of the Corporation, ... The factors to be considered
in granting or withholding the consent of the Corporation under this subsection shall be those enumerated in
section 6 of this Act."

"Sec. 6.   The factors........to be considered by the Board of Directors........shall be the following: The financial
history and condition of the bank, the adequacy of its capital structure, its future earnings prospects, the general
character of its management, the convenience and needs of the community to be served by the bank, and whether
or not its corporate powers are consistent with the purposes of this Act."

In support of this Application, the following statements, representations, and information upon the several factors enumerated in Section 6 of the Federal Deposit Insurance Act are submitted for the purpose of inducing the Board of Directors
of the Federal Deposit Insurance Corporation to grant its prior written consent to the establishment of the Proposed
Branch:

---

*Mutual savings bank without trust or insurance powers; mutual savings bank with trust powers, but without insurance powers; mutual savings
bank with insurance powers, but without trust powers; or, mutual savings bank with both trust and insurance powers.

1

FORM 85 REVISED 5-1-52

(1) FINANCIAL HISTORY AND CONDITION

The following is a statement of the assets and liabilities of the Applicant Bank as of the date of this Application:

S A M P L E

The name and address of the main office and of each existing branch and the total amount of deposits arising as a result of the operation of the main office and of each existing branch as of the date of this Application are shown in the following schedule:

It is anticipated that a normal deposit volume of approximately $...will be obtained by the Proposed Branch within.......................................months after its establishment.

The following is a detailed description of the premises to be occupied by the Proposed Branch. It includes name of owner and annual rental, if by lease; date of construction, original cost, price to be paid, and from whom acquired, if by purchase; or the estimated cost, if new construction.

*The Proposed Branch is to be established as a result of a merger or consolidation of the Applicant Bank with.....................

...., ...
            Name of Bank   City
...., or the purchase of assets from, and the assumption of liabilities of, said bank.
   State
There are attached copies of all (proposed) contracts and documents to be used in effecting said transaction together with a statement of the assets and liabilities of the merged or purchased bank. Other information essential to a full understanding of the transaction is as follows:

(2) ADEQUACY OF CAPITAL STRUCTURE

The capital structure of the Applicant Bank, as of the date of this Application, is as follows:

	Number of shares	Par value per share	Amount
Preferred capital..			
Common capital..			
Surplus..			
Undivided profits..			
Other segregations of the capital account..........................			
Total capital structure			

The capital structure of the Applicant Bank will be increased as follows prior to the establishment of the Proposed Branch:

The capital requirements of State law relative to the operation of the Applicant Bank, the Proposed Branch, and other existing branches, as contemplated in this Application are as follows:

The Applicant Bank will at all times maintain adequate total capital accounts in relation to the true value of its total assets.

*This paragraph need not be complied with, of course, unless the Proposed Branch is established as a result of any of the transactions therein mentioned.

2

FORM 82 REVISED 5-1-52

(3) FUTURE EARNINGS PROSPECTS

It is the opinion of the undersigned that the earnings of the proposed Bank will be sufficient within a reasonable period after commencement of business as an insured bank, to cover all operating expenses, losses, and charge-offs and to provide a reasonable return to shareholders.

There follows a statement of the current operating earnings and expenses of the Predecessor Institution for the last calendar year or for the twelve months ending..; or, if there is no Predecessor Institution, there follows a statement of estimated current operating earnings and expenses of the proposed Bank for the first twelve months following the beginning of business:

Current Operating Earnings	*Current Operating Expenses*
(a) Interest and discount on loans . . . . . ————	(a) Interest on time and savings deposits . . . ————
(b) Interest and dividends on securities . . . ————	(b) Interest and discount on borrowings . . . ————
(c) Commissions, fees, and collection, exchange, and service charges . . . . ————	(c) Salaries and wages . . . . ————
(d) Other current operating earnings . . . . ————	(d) Taxes (other than on net income) . . . . ————
Gross Current Operating Earnings . . . . . ————	(e) Other current operating expenses . . . . ————
	Total Current Operating Expenses . . . . . ————

Annual charges for regular depreciation to be taken on bank premises will approximate ....% of original cost. Annual charges for depreciation on furniture and fixtures will average approximately ....% of original costs to Bank. Annual charges for regular depreciation on bank premises of $............................ and furniture and fixtures of $............................ are included in the above statement under item (e).

(4) MANAGEMENT

The proposed directors and officers are listed below. Following the name of each of the proposed officers is a brief resume or outline of his past business and banking experience and other qualifications as well as a brief statement of his proposed duties in connection with the operation of the Bank.

Name, address, and occupation	Age	Title and Duties	Net worth	Annual salary	Par value of stock to be subscribed	
					Preferred	Common

No changes are contemplated in the proposed directorate or active management of the Bank, within the first year of operation, with the following possible exceptions:

None of the proposed directors, officers or employees of the proposed Bank has been convicted of any criminal offense involving dishonesty or a breach of trust.

There is detailed below (a) the indebtedness of each of the above Directors and Officers and their unincorporated companies to any Predecessor Institution, (b) the indebtedness to any Predecessor Institution of corporations in which any of the above Directors or Officers are substantially interested, (c) securities held by any Predecessor Institution issued by corporations in which any of the above Directors or Officers are substantially interested, and (d) the indebtedness or portions thereof of others to any Predecessor Institution, collateralled by securities issued by corporations in which any of the above Directors or Officers are substantially interested: (the term indebtedness includes both direct and indirect liabilities).

There is listed below each prospective shareholder (excluding Directors and Officers) subscribing 10 per centum or more of the aggregate par value of stock to be issued, together with the aggregate par value of common or preferred stock each will purchase.

The Applicant Bank will at all times maintain sufficient surety bond coverage on its active officers and employees to conform with generally accepted banking practices.

FORM 85 REVISED 5-1-52

(5) CONVENIENCE AND NEEDS OF COMMUNITY

COPY

Existing banks and branches of banks located in same city or town as the Proposed Branch and existing banks and branches of banks located within a radius of twenty-five miles of the Proposed Branch are as follows:

Name of bank or branch	Location	Population	Approximate deposits	Distance from the Proposed Branch

The approximate population of the town or city of the Proposed Branch is.................... The approximate population of the trade area to be served by the Proposed Branch is................................

The principal industries of the community of the Proposed Branch are:

Name	Type	Approximate number of employees	Approximate annual payroll	Approximate annual sales

The principal agricultural, mineral, and other products of the trade area to be served are:

The approximate average annual value of the above products during the past three years is:

Other supporting information relative to the factor of convenience and needs of the community is as follows:

(6) CONSISTENCY OF CORPORATE POWERS

The Applicant Bank is organized pursuant to...

(Give citation of State statutory provisions)

There is attached hereto a true copy of the Articles of Incorporation or Association of the Applicant Bank, together with all amendments thereto. (If previously submitted only subsequent amendments are to be attached.)

It is agreed that the Applicant Bank will not, except as incidental to the usual functions of a bank, guarantee mortgages, mortage or other participation certificates, or real estate land titles, or obligate itself under any contract of suretyship or guaranty.

4

FORM 85M REVISED 5-1-52

RESOLUTION OF BOARD OF TRUSTEES OF APPLICANT BANK

C O P Y

The Board of Trustees of the Applicant Bank at a meeting duly called and held on...
S A M P L E
adopted the following Resolution:

"WHEREAS, it is the sense of this meeting that application should be made on behalf of this Bank to the Federal Deposit Insurance Corporation for written consent to establish a branch at..
(Street Address)
....in accordance with the provisions
(City or Town)   (State)
of the Federal Deposit Insurance Act;

NOW, THEREFORE, IT IS RESOLVED, That the President or Vice-President and the Treasurer or Secretary of this Bank are hereby authorized and directed to make application on behalf of this Bank to the Federal Deposit Insurance Corporation to establish a branch at..
(Street Address)   (City or Town)   (State)
and to submit to the Federal Deposit Insurance Corporation in connection therewith information on the several factors enumerated under Section 6 of the Federal Deposit Insurance Act for the purpose of inducing the Board of Directors of the Federal Deposit Insurance Corporation to grant its written consent to the establishment of a branch as indicated in this Resolution."

The above Resolution has not been rescinded or modified and has been duly entered on the minute book of the Applicant Bank.

It is requested that an Examiner of the Federal Deposit Insurance Corporation be assigned to conduct the necessary investigation or examination.

Date:... ....
(Name and Location of Applicant Bank)

(SEAL)   By..
(President or Vice-President)

Attest:

....
(Treasurer or Secretary)

CERTIFICATE OF TRUSTEES OF APPLICANT BANK

The undersigned, constituting a majority of the Trustees of the Applicant Bank, do hereby certify and state, jointly and severally, that they have read this Application and all statements, representations, and information contained therein and that said statements, representations, and information are true and correct to the best of their knowledge and belief and are submitted for the purpose of inducing the Federal Deposit Insurance Corporation to grant its prior written consent to the establishment or relocation of a branch as provided in this Application.

Date:..

Signed: Address:

....

....

....

....

....

....

INFORMATION FOR APPLICANT

1. Any signing Trustee desiring to qualify his certificate may do so by attaching hereto any statement which may be required to make his certificate accurate.
2. Schedules or inserts may be attached to this Application wherever the space provided for certain information is insufficient. Such attached schedules or inserts are to be regarded as a part of this Application and must be signed by the Trustees. All schedules or inserts should preferably be on paper the same size as this page. Applications are to be securely bound at the top of the page.
3. This Application is to be executed in quadruplicate, three signed Applications to be forwarded to the Supervising Examiner of the Federal Deposit Insurance Corporation for the Federal Deposit Insurance District in which the Applicant Bank is located and the other Application is to be retained in the files of the Applicant Bank.
4. If in any instance it is not clear as to what information is necessary to complete this Application, a letter to the Supervising Examiner of the Corporation for the District in which the Applicant Bank is located will bring a prompt and informative reply.

5

FORM 85 *Application to be filed by a Commercial Bank.*

FORM 82 REVISED 5-1-52

Application of Proposed Bank for Federal Deposit Insurance

FEDERAL DEPOSIT INSURANCE CORPORATION
WASHINGTON, D. C.

SIRS:

We, the undersigned prospective incorporators, being natural persons and of lawful age, intend to organize a State banking corporation, under the title of " ....
.... "

to be located at ...., County of ....,
(Street Address—City or Town)

State of ...., pursuant to ....

....
(Give citation of State statutory provisions)

We hereby make application to the Federal Deposit Insurance Corporation on behalf of said proposed Bank to become, upon its organization, an insured bank under the provisions of the Federal Deposit Insurance Act. The general character or type of business which will be exercised by the Bank will be: (Check all appropriate items) ( ) Commercial banking; ( ) Savings banking; ( ) Industrial banking; ( ) Trust business; ( ) Cash depository; ( ) Others. Specify..........

....

It is understood that the Board of Directors of the Federal Deposit Insurance Corporation in applying the factors set out in Section 6 of the Federal Deposit Insurance Act to this Application, will consider the Application only with respect to the general character or type of business above stated and that the Bank will not engage in any other business without the prior written consent of the Corporation.

It is further understood that insurance under the Federal Deposit Insurance Act will not become effective (a) until the proposed Bank has been incorporated and authorized to engage in the business of receiving deposits, (b) until the Board of Directors of the Bank has adopted a resolution (Form 82A) ratifying and confirming the action of these incorporators in making this Application with supporting information, (c) until the Bank has fulfilled such requirements, if any, as may be imposed by the Federal Deposit Insurance Corporation as a condition of its approval of this Application, and (d) until the Bank has been notified that its membership in said Corporation has been approved.

We have, in connection with this Application, read the following provisions of the Federal Deposit Insurance Act which govern the admission of banks to membership in the Federal Deposit Insurance Corporation, namely:

"Sec. 5. Subject to the provisions of this Act, . . . any State nonmember bank, upon application to and examination by the Corporation and approval by the Board of Directors, may become an insured bank. Before approving the application of any such State nonmember bank, the Board of Directors shall give consideration to the factors enumerated in section 6 and shall determine, upon the basis of a thorough examination of such bank, that its assets in excess of its capital requirements are adequate to enable it to meet all its liabilities to depositors and other creditors as shown by the books of the bank."

"Sec. 6. The factors . . . to be considered by the Board of Directors under section 5 shall be the following: The financial history and condition of the bank, the adequacy of its capital structure, its future earnings prospects, the general character of its management, the convenience and needs of the community to be served by the bank, and whether or not its corporate powers are consistent with the purposes of this Act."

In support of this Application, we hereby make the following statements and representations and submit the following information upon the several factors enumerated in Section 6 of the Federal Deposit Insurance Act for the purpose of inducing the Board of Directors of the Federal Deposit Insurance Corporation to approve the proposed Bank for membership in said Corporation, and we hereby request that an Examiner of said Corporation be assigned to make the necessary investigation or examination:

1

FORM 82 REVISED 5-1-52

(1) FINANCIAL HISTORY AND CONDITION

A statement of the estimated assets and liabilities of the proposed Bank, as of the beginning of business, is as follows:

S A M P L E

The following is a detailed description of the premises to be occupied by the Bank. It includes name of owner and annual rental, if by lease; date of construction, original cost, price to be paid, and from whom acquired, if by purchase; or the estimated cost, if new construction.

There is set forth below a brief history of the operations of any banking institution the assets and liabilities of which are to be assumed in whole or in part by the proposed Bank, such banking institution being hereinafter referred to as Predecessor Institution. This history includes the date of organization and full information on any mergers, consolidations, conversions, reorganizations, recapitalization programs, guaranties or guaranty bonds executed, capital contributions, liability or deposit assumptions, deposit waivers, deposit deferment or restriction agreements, subordinations of claims or deposits, and so forth, which have occurred during the past twenty years.

(2) ADEQUACY OF CAPITAL STRUCTURE

The *paid-in* capital structure, as of the beginning of business, will be as follows:

	Number of shares	Par value per share	Amount
Preferred capital			
Common capital			
Surplus			
Undivided profits			
Other segregations of the capital account			
		Total capital structure	

The capital requirements of State law relative to organization of a bank at the location and with powers as proposed are as follows:

It is estimated that after the beginning of business the Bank will have a normal deposit volume as follows: One year, $................................: two years, $................................: three years, $................................

The applicant Bank will at all times maintain adequate total capital accounts in relation to the true value of its total assets.

The proposed Bank upon organization will not refinance, either directly or indirectly, any loan, advance, or credit extension made to any prospective shareholder by any existing financial institution or by others, if such loan, advance, or credit extension was originally made to the prospective shareholder to obtain funds to purchase stock in the proposed Bank.

2

FORM 65M REVISED 5-1-52

(3) FUTURE EARNINGS PROSPECTS

COPY

There follows a statement of the current operating earnings and expenses of the Applicant Bank or its Predecessor Institution during the last calendar year or for the twelve month period ending..; or, if the Applicant Bank has been recently organized and has no Predecessor Institution, there follows a pro forma statement of anticipated current operating earnings and expenses for the first twelve months following membership of Applicant Bank in the Federal Deposit Insurance Corporation:

Current Operating Earnings		*Current Operating Expenses*	
(a) Interest and discount on loans	_____	(a) Interest (Dividends) on time and savings deposits	_____
(b) Interest and dividends on securities . . .	_____	(b) Interest and discount on borrowings . . .	_____
(c) Commissions, fees, and collection, exchange, and service charges	_____	(c) Salaries and wages	_____
(d) Other current operating earnings	_____	(d) Taxes (Other than on net income)	_____
Gross Current Operating Earnings	_____	(e) Other current operating expenses	_____
		Total Current Operating Expenses	_____

The following is an itemization of current operating expenses on a yearly basis which will result from the operation of the Proposed Branch:

It is the opinion of the undersigned that the operating earnings which will result from the operation of the Proposed Branch will be sufficiently in excess of the estimated current operating expenses listed above to justify the operation of the Proposed Branch.

(4) MANAGEMENT

The proposed officers of the Proposed Branch are listed below with information in regard to each. Following the name of each of the proposed officers is a brief resume or outline of his past business or banking experience and other qualifications as well as a brief statement of his duties and responsibilities in connection with the operation of the Proposed Branch.

Name, address and occupation	Age	Title and duties	Annual salary

Officers of the Proposed Branch will have the following authority in connection with the granting of loans and discounts and extending credit:

A brief summary of the supervision and control which will be exercised by the officials of Applicant Bank over the activities of the Proposed Branch is as follows:

The Applicant Bank will at all times maintain sufficient surety bond coverage on its active officers and employees to conform with generally accepted banking practices.

3

FORM 65M REVISED 5-1-52

(5) CONVENIENCE AND NEEDS OF COMMUNITY
SAMPLE

Existing banks and branches of banks located in same city or town as the Proposed Branch and existing banks and branches of banks located within a radius of twenty-five miles of the Proposed Branch are as follows:

Name of bank or branch	Location	Population	Approximate deposits	Distance from the Proposed Branch

The approximate population of the town or city of the Proposed Branch is.................. The approximate population of the trade area to be served by the Proposed Branch is...............................

The principal industries of the community of the Proposed Branch are:

Name	Type	Approximate number of employees	Approximate annual payroll	Approximate annual sales

The principal agricultural, mineral, and other products of the trade area to be served are:

The approximate average annual value of the above products during the past three years is:

Other supporting information relative to the factor of convenience and needs of the community is as follows:

(6) CONSISTENCY OF CORPORATE POWERS

The Applicant Bank is organized pursuant to...
....
(Give citation of State statutory provisions)

There is attached hereto a true copy of the Articles of Incorporation or Association of the Applicant Bank, together with all amendments thereto. (If previously submitted only subsequent amendments are to be attached.)

It is agreed that the Applicant Bank will not, except as incidental to the usual functions of a bank, guarantee mortgages, mortgage or other participation certificates, or real estate land titles, or obligate itself under any contract of suretyship or guaranty.

4

FORM 82A REVISED 12-1-50

CERTIFICATE OF ADOPTION OF RESOLUTION

The undersigned,..................................... S A M P L E ....and...
_____(President or Vice-President)_____(Cashier or Secretary)

of the.., do hereby certify that the fol-
_____(Name of Bank)_____(Street Address)_____(City or Town and State)

lowing is a true and correct copy of a resolution duly adopted by the Board of Directors of the said Bank at a meeting of

said Board regularly called and held on...; and entered in the minutes of that meeting:
_____(Date)

"WHEREAS, there was submitted to the Federal Deposit Insurance Corporation an APPLICATION OF PRO-
POSED BANK FOR FEDERAL DEPOSIT INSURANCE (Form 82) duly executed and forwarded to the Federal

Deposit Insurance Corporation on..,

by Messrs.., ...,

...., ...,

and..., prospective incorporators of the

...., then in the process of
_____(Name of Bank)_____(City or Town and State)

organization; and

"WHEREAS, said Application was made by the prospective incorporators on behalf of the Bank, upon the
understanding that such insurance was not to become effective (a) until the proposed Bank had been in-
porated and authorized to engage in the business of receiving deposits, (b) until the Board of Directors of
the Bank had adopted a resolution ratifying and confirming the action of said incorporators in making said
Application with supporting information, and (c) until the Bank had fulfilled such requirements, if any, as
might be imposed by the Federal Deposit Insurance Corporation as a condition of its approval of said
Application, and (d) until the Bank had been approved for membership in said Corporation and so notified;
and

"WHEREAS, the Bank has been duly incorporated and chartered as a State bank and authorized to
receive deposits and do a banking business by the proper State Authority;

"NOW, THEREFORE, IT IS RESOLVED, that the Board of Directors of the Bank hereby approves the said
action of the prospective incorporators of the Bank in preparing and presenting to the Federal Deposit
Insurance Corporation said Application, and hereby ratifies and confirms the same, with the same force and
effect as if said Application had been made in behalf of the Bank by this Board;

"RESOLVED, that a true copy of said Application shall be and the same is hereby made a part of the minutes
of this meeting; that all of the written statements and representations therein made by said incorporators
and all of the written information therein contained, submitted by them upon the several factors enumerated
in Section 6 of the Federal Deposit Insurance Act to the Federal Deposit Insurance Corporation for the purpose of inducing said Corporation to accept this Bank, when organized, as a member thereof, be and the
same are hereby adopted, ratified, and confirmed as statements, representations, and information submitted by this Board, except as hereinafter noted, with like effect as though made and submitted by it:

RESOLVED, that the President or Vice-President and Cashier or Secretary of this Bank are hereby authorized and directed to prepare and transmit to the Federal Deposit Insurance Corporation, Washington,
D. C., the following documents, properly certified by them:

(1) One copy of this Resolution;

(2) A copy (if not heretofore submitted) of the Articles of Incorporation or Association of the
Bank; and,

(3) A copy (if not heretofore submitted) of the License or other instrument authorizing the Bank
to engage in the business of receiving deposits."

Date:.. ....
_____(Name and Location of Applicant Bank)

(Seal)

By:...
_____(President or Vice-President)

Attest:...
_____(Cashier or Secretary)

Notes

II

1 *American Banker,* July 11, 1958, pp. 1–8.
2 Annual Reports, Federal Deposit Insurance Corporation, 1940–1959. These figures include savings banks.
3 "Branch Banking in the U.S., 1939 and 1949," *Federal Reserve Bulletin,* July, 1950.
4 "Changes in the Number and Class of Operating Banks and Branches in the United States," Annual Reports, FDIC, 1946–1959, including savings banks.
5 Annual Report, Federal Home Loan Bank Board, 1958.
6 *Ibid.,* p. 44.
7 All dollar comparisons are in current dollars, which include price increases.
8 FDIC.
9 Rand McNally International Bankers Directory (Chicago, Ill.: Rand McNally & Co.; published twice a year).
10 *Branch Banking Studies,* Case History No. 1 by Spencer Weart.

III

1 Annual Report, FDIC, 1959, Table 113.
2 Benjamin H. Beckhart (editor), *Banking Systems* (New York: Columbia University Press, 1954), p. 849.
3 Conversely, the same legislation placed a penalizing tax on the outstanding currency of state banks.
4 Annual Report, FDIC, 1959, Table 102.

5 Annual Report, FDIC, 1959, Table 102.
6 *American Banker,* Jan. 9, 1957, pp. 1–5.
7 Jointly with the Federal Home Loan Bank in the district in question.
8 Revised Statutes of the United States, Sec. 5168.
    Donald M. Hoffman, *A Study of Bank Chartering Procedures* (Graduate School of Banking, 1957), pp. 38–39.
    Michie on Banks and Banking (Charlottesville, Va.: Michie Company Publishers), Vol. I, p. 15.
9 Annual Report, FDIC, 1959, Tables 101, 108.
10 National Bank Act, 1954, Chap. III, Sec. 468.
11 *American Banker,* Jan. 9, 1957, p. 1.
12 Annual Reports, FDIC, 1946–1957.

IV

1 For a detailed discussion, see Appendix A in *Marketing Research for Banks* (Chicago: Association of Reserve City Bankers, 1959).
2 Wendell August, Jr., "An Informative Case History in Branch Location," *Banking,* December, 1955.
3 John O. Chappell, "How Banks Can Use Census Data," *Burroughs Clearing House,* May, 1950.
4 Frequently the Census Bureau has data in greater depth which have not been published. If so, it may be obtained for legitimate purposes.
5 "1957 Survey of Consumer Finances," *Federal Reserve Bulletin,* June, 1957, pp. 563–566.
6 Spencer A. Weart, "A Method of Finding an Area's Deposit Potential," *Banking,* March, 1957.
7 Reference Book of Dun & Bradstreet, Inc., New York (published quarterly).
8 Statement Studies (Robert Morris Associates, Nat'l. Assn. of Bank Loan Officers and Credit Men; Philadelphia, Pa.; published yearly).

V

1 All the cases are actual, the data have been disguised to protect the banks in question.
2 "The Financial Position of Consumers," *Federal Reserve Bulletin,* July, 1959, p. 708.

VII

1 Data on new bank attainments is confidential and has been disguised. However, outside sources of information are cited where possible.
2 Municipal Credit Survey (New York: Dun & Bradstreet, Inc.; published yearly).

3 Local post-office records.
4 State Industrial Directory.
5 Survey of Buying Power (New York: Sales Management; published yearly).
6 State Industrial Directory.

VIII

1 Sales Management.
2 City and County Data Book.

X

1 There will be some but it cannot be relied upon.
2 These figures were compiled by Spencer Weart, banking consultant, New York City, as a matter of general background to his work. They have not been previously published.
3 Statistics on the Savings Market (New York: Savings and Mortgage Division, American Bankers Association; 1960 ed.).

Appendix III

1 United States Code, Chap. 12, Secs. 1814(b), 1815.
2 United States Code, Chap. 12, Secs. 1814(b), 1816.
3 United States Code, Chap. 12, Sec. 1828(d).
4 Paton's Digest, Vol. I, p. 507, also *Federal Reserve Bulletin,* December, 1940, p. 1267.
5 Paton, p. 507; Federal Reserve Act, Sec. 19; Paton *Supplement,* Sec. 25.
6 United States Code, Chap. 12, Sec. 36(c)(d).
7 United States Code, Chap. 12, Secs. 84, 284(k), 371.
8 Paton, Vol. I, p. 507.
9 United States Code, Chap. 45, Sec. 19.
10 Paton, Vol. I, p. 508.
11 Paton, Vol. II, pp. 1530, 1538.
12 United States Code, Chap. 12, Sec. 548.

Bibliography

BOOKS

Benjamin H. Beckhart (editor). *Banking Systems*. New York: Columbia University Press, 1954.

Michie on Banks and Banking. Charlottesville, Va.: Michie Company Law Publishers, 1944, Vol. 1.

Studenski and Krooss. *Financial History of the United States*. New York: McGraw-Hill Book Co., 1952.

THESES

Thomas M. Ainslie. *Prerequisite for Selecting an Urban Branch Location*. Graduate School of Banking, 1952.

Donald M. Hoffman. *A Study of Bank Chartering Procedures*. Graduate School of Banking, 1957.

REPORTS, PAMPHLETS, AND BOOKLETS

Municipal Credit Survey. New York: Dun & Bradstreet, Inc. (published yearly).

Rand McNally International Bankers Directory. Chicago: Rand McNally & Company (published twice a year).

Reference Book. New York: Dun & Bradstreet, Inc. (published quarterly).

Statement Studies, Robert Morris Associates. Philadelphia: National Association of Bank Loan Officers and Credit Men (published yearly).

Survey of Buying Power. New York: Sales Management, Inc. (published yearly).

PERIODICALS

American Banker, July 11, 1958, and Jan. 9, 1957.

Robert H. Armstrong. "Banking Expansion—New Frontiers Ahead." *Urban Land Institute,* May, 1959.

Wendell August. "An Informative Case History in Branch Location." *Banking,* December, 1955.

"Branch Banking in the United States, 1939 and 1949." *Federal Reserve Bulletin,* July, 1950.

John O. Chappell. "How Banks Can Use Census Data." *Burroughs Clearing House,* May, 1950.

"How to Select a Site for a Branch." *The Girard Letter.* Girard Trust Corn Exchange Bank, Philadelphia, Pa., December, 1957.

"1957 Survey of Consumer Finances." *Federal Reserve Bulletin,* June–August, 1957.

"Statistics on the Savings Market." 1960 Edition Savings and Mortgage Division, American Bankers Association.

Spencer A. Weart. "A Method of Finding an Area's Deposit Potential." *Banking,* March, 1957.

GOVERNMENT DOCUMENTS AND REPORTS

Annual Reports. Federal Deposit Insurance Corporation, Washington, D.C., 1940–1957.

Annual Reports. Federal Home Loan Bank Board, Washington, D.C.

County and City Data Book. Bureau of the Census, U.S. Department of Commerce, 1956 Edition.

Marketing Research Activities of Banks. Association of Reserve City Bankers, Chicago, June, 1959.

Statistical Abstract. Bureau of the Census, U.S. Department of Commerce, 1958 Edition.

"Survey of Consumer Finances." Annually in various issues of *Federal Reserve Bulletin.* Board of Governors of Federal Reserve System. (Surveys by Survey Research Center, University of Michigan.)

LAW COMPILATIONS

Paton's Digest, 1944, Vol. I.
Paton's Digest, 1944, Vol. II.
Paton's Supplement, Sec. 25.

STATUTES

Revised Statutes of the United States, Sec. 5168.
National Bank Act, 1954, Chaps. III and IV.
12 U.S.C., Secs. 36, 84, 284, 371, 548, 1814–1816, 1828.
45 U.S.C., Sec. 19.